# Derrick Rose

**by Adam Woog**

**LUCENT BOOKS**

*A part of Gale, Cengage Learning*

GALE
CENGAGE Learning™

Detroit • New York • San Francisco • New Haven, Conn • Waterville, Maine • London

## GALE
### CENGAGE Learning™

**LIBRARY OF CONGRESS CATALOGING-IN-PUBLICATION DATA**

Woog, Adam, 1953-
  Derrick Rose / by Adam Woog.
      p. cm. -- (People in the news)
  Includes bibliographical references and index.
  ISBN 978-1-4205-0233-6 (hardcover)
  1. Rose, Derrick. 2. Basketball players--United States--Biography--
Juvenile literature. I. Title.
  GV884.R619W6 2010
  796.323092--dc22
  [B]
                                                        2009050414

Lucent Books
27500 Drake Rd.
Farmington Hills, MI 48331


ISBN-13: 978-1-4205-0233-6
ISBN-10: 1-4205-0233-6

*Once again: This is for Leah,
my star basketball player.*

Printed in the United States of America
1 2 3 4 5 6 7 14 13 12 11 10

Printed by Bang Printing, Brainerd, MN, 1ˢᵗ Ptg., 05/2010

# Contents

Fame and celebrity are alluring. People are drawn to those who walk in fame's spotlight, whether they are known for great accomplishments or for notorious deeds. The lives of the famous pique public interest and attract attention, perhaps because their experiences seem in some ways so different from, yet in other ways so similar to, our own.

Newspapers, magazines, and television regularly capitalize on this fascination with celebrity by running profiles of famous people. For example, television programs such as *Entertainment Tonight* devote all of their programming to stories about entertainment and entertainers. Magazines such as *People* fill their pages with stories of the private lives of famous people. Even newspapers, newsmagazines, and television news frequently delve into the lives of well-known personalities. Despite the number of articles and programs, few provide more than a superficial glimpse at their subjects.

Lucent's People in the News series offers young readers a deeper look into the lives of today's newsmakers, the influences that have shaped them, and the impact they have had in their fields of endeavor and on other people's lives. The subjects of the series hail from many disciplines and walks of life. They include authors, musicians, athletes, political leaders, entertainers, entrepreneurs, and others who have made a mark on modern life and who, in many cases, will continue to do so for years to come.

These biographies are more than factual chronicles. Each book emphasizes the contributions, accomplishments, or deeds that have brought fame or notoriety to the individual and shows how that person has influenced modern life. Authors portray their subjects in a realistic, unsentimental light. For example, Bill Gates—the cofounder and chief executive officer of the software giant Microsoft—has been instrumental in making personal computers the most vital tool of the modern age. Few dispute his business savvy, his perseverance, or his technical expertise, yet critics say he is ruthless in his dealings with competitors and driven more by his desire to maintain Microsoft's dominance in the computer industry than by an interest in furthering technology.

In these books, young readers will encounter inspiring stories about real people who achieved success despite enormous obstacles. Oprah Winfrey—the most powerful, most watched, and wealthiest woman on television today—spent the first six years of her life in the care of her grandparents while her unwed mother sought work and a better life elsewhere. Her adolescence was colored by promiscuity, pregnancy at age fourteen, rape, and sexual abuse.

Each author documents and supports his or her work with an array of primary and secondary source quotations taken from diaries, letters, speeches, and interviews. All quotes are footnoted to show readers exactly how and where biographers derive their information and provide guidance for further research. The quotations enliven the text by giving readers eyewitness views of the life and accomplishments of each person covered in the People in the News series.

In addition, each book in the series includes photographs, annotated bibliographies, timelines, and comprehensive indexes. For both the casual reader and the student researcher, the People in the News series offers insight into the lives of today's newsmakers—people who shape the way we live, work, and play in the modern age.

# A Basketball Phenomenon

Derrick Rose is a genuine basketball phenomenon. As a high school student at Simeon Career Academy in Chicago, Illinois, the point guard twice led an elite team to victory in the state championships. During the year that he spent at the University of Memphis, he had another outstanding season and emerged as one of the most exciting young players in the country.

Then Rose's dream came true. While still in his teens, he was chosen as the first pick in the 2008 National Basketball Associa-

## A "Lights-On Guy"

Ben Howland, the University of California, Los Angeles, basketball coach, is one of the many coaches who admire and appreciate Rose's talents. He remarks, "What I like most about Derrick Rose is that when the lights are on, he takes his game to a different level. The significance of the game raises his game to a higher level. He's a big-game, big-time, lights-on guy. That's when he shines best. Those guys are few and far between."

Quoted in Andy Katz, "Rose 'Chases Greatness' with a Passion for Winning," ESPN.com, June 20, 2008. http://sports.espn.go.com/nba/draft2008/columns/story?id=3452587.

*With the support of his family, Derrick Rose was able to avoid bad influences and become a professional player with the Chicago Bulls.*

tion (NBA) draft. The organization that chose him, the Chicago Bulls, was his hometown team, the one he grew up watching. This powerhouse franchise had been the headquarters of superstars like Michael Jordan, Dennis Rodman, and Scottie Pippen.

## Michael Jordan in an Iron Man Suit

During his rookie year with the legendary Chicago Bulls, Rose confidently assumed his role as team leader, turned the struggling team around, and brought Chicago to within reach of a national championship. And the 6 foot, 3 inch (1.9m), 190-pound (86kg) star accomplished all of that before he turned twenty-one.

During that season—and in every other before and after it—Rose demonstrated the skills that have made him an outstanding player. On offense, he never slacks off, relentlessly looking for opportunities to attack. He has a genius for seeing the entire court at once. He can slip through traffic, drive around and through defenders, finish at the rim to sink shot after shot—often with a crowd-pleasing dunk—and make it look almost easy.

## "The Only Answer"

**W**hen asked about what has helped him succeed in addition to his family, Rose mentions his deep religious faith. According to Rose, his faith has helped him be a better person. He remarked to a reporter, "God. That's the only answer I [can come] up with. I guess because I've been trying to do everything right. I'm not treating people wrong, I've been on the positive side, doing everything I need to do. Just trying to be a good person. I guess that's why this is happening to me."

Quoted in Scoop Jackson, "The Rose That Rose from Concrete," ESPN.com, April 15, 2009. http://sports.espn.go.com/chicago/columns/story?columnist=jackson_scoop&id= 4070218.

In his role as the leader on the court, he confidently controls the tempo of the game and directs his teammates' offensive play. As a defender, he can get low and anticipate what his opponent tries to do. And he is also generous—often, if it creates a play that will benefit the team as a whole, he will pass the ball rather than try to rack up a showy basket himself.

This unselfish attitude typifies Rose's passion for winning at any cost. He comments, "I just hate losing [and] I'm really competitive. . . . No matter what it is, I'll do it to win. Winning is the goal for me."[1]

Finally, Rose has almost superhuman speed and agility. Bill Self, the head basketball coach at the University of Kansas, recalls how he once saw the guard grab a defensive rebound and take the ball to the offensive goal in just three dribbles. That is roughly 31 feet (9.4m) per dribble, which is an amazing achievement. One writer asked about this feat, "Could even Michael Jordan in his prime—and in an Iron Man suit—have done that?"[2]

## "I Could Have Followed That Path Too"

Rose has developed the skills that make him one of the hottest players in the NBA, and has remained modest about his achievements, despite a number of potential dangers. He grew up in Chicago in a rough neighborhood called Englewood, an area that has had more than its share of misfortunes.

Fortunately, although he spent his childhood in this rough neighborhood, he never succumbed to the temptations of drugs or gang life. Rose recalls, "Just living in Englewood is tough, trust me. It's really tough. I had friends dropping out in grammar school. I couldn't believe it. Grammar school. And I could have followed that path too."[3]

One big reason why Rose evaded that path was due to the constant support of his family—his mother, Brenda, and his three older brothers, Dwayne, Reggie, and Allan. Rose's father does not participate in his life. All through Rose's life, the family

# Just the Facts

**H**ere are some of Derrick Rose's vital statisics:

Full name: Derrick Martell Rose
Birthday: October 4, 1988
Birthplace: Chicago, Illinois
Height: 6 feet 3 inches (1.9m)
Weight: 190 pounds (86kg)
Position: Point guard
High school: Simeon Career Academy, Chicago, Illinois
College: University of Memphis, Tennessee
Professional Team: Chicago Bulls
Jersey Number: 1

has fostered his talent and protected the youngest Rose from the dangers of the street. By all accounts, he is succeeding in the high-pressure world of professional sports thanks to their guidance and his own inner strength.

Rose's positive attitude has helped him become an example to others. Robert Smith, who was the point guard's coach in high school, comments, "Everyone's not going to make it out of this neighborhood. Some kids here have real issues. But Derrick has put a different light on things. Through all the negativity, he's shown these kids they're not limited by where they come from."[4] Of course, the young athletes and fans looking to Rose for inspiration are not just those living in his home neighborhood. Nor are all of them growing up in difficult environments. They come from everywhere, and from all kinds of backgrounds.

Still, they have one thing in common. They admire Derrick Rose's athletic skills and positive attitude. The path to developing these characteristics began in Rose's home neighborhood of Englewood.

# Chapter 1

# Growing Up in Englewood

Derrick Martell Rose was born on October 4, 1988. His mother was a single parent who worked as a teacher's assistant. The Rose family—Dwayne, Reggie, and Allan, plus their mother and Derrick—lived in a modest house at West Seventy-third and South Paulina streets on the South Side of Chicago.

In many ways, Rose's early years were typical of boys his age. He attended a public elementary school called Beasley Academic Center. When not studying or doing chores around the house, both of which Brenda Rose strictly enforced, Derrick, his brothers, and their friends kept busy with typical kid activities—especially hoops.

## Chicago

Chicago, where Rose grew up, can be, in many ways, a good place to live. The third-largest city in the United States, it has great universities and world-class museums, and it is one of the nation's centers for business and manufacturing. Its cultural scene is enlivened by the presence of many diverse ethnic groups, including African American, Polish, Italian, and Jewish communities.

Furthermore, the city has a large base of sports fans devoted to its professional teams: the Bears (football), the Cubs and the White Sox (baseball), the Blackhawks (hockey), and the Bulls (basketball). All of these teams have been home to superior athletes, notably the legendary Bulls player Michael Jordan.

*Derrick Rose poses with his family after winning NBA Rookie of the Year. Along with their mom, brothers Reggie, left, and Dwayne, far right, supported Derrick's NBA dream.*

But Chicago also has its negative aspects. The city and its residents have a reputation for toughness. In earlier decades, the city was famous as the home territory of ruthless gangsters like Al Capone. Even today, it has crime, drug abuse, and poverty.

## "Now, It's Crazy"

In this city of tough neighborhoods, Englewood is one of its toughest. Englewood is also one of the poorest areas of the city, with a high incidence of problems such as unemployment and abandoned buildings.

Nonetheless, Rose has some positive memories of growing up in Englewood. For instance, he can remember having a good time sitting on the porches of his friends' houses and playing hoops on hot summer evenings—at least until his mother made him come home. He recalls, "When I was 10, I didn't know a neighborhood [that was] greater. . . . At the park, it was just positive stuff. Now, it's crazy. You have kids dropping out of school at 13 and everyone has a gun. They don't care who's around when they go shooting."[5]

## Playing for Beasley

Right from the beginning, Derrick Rose was an excellent athlete. He was tall and strong for his age. In fact, even at birth he was not a lightweight—as a newborn he had tipped the scales at a whopping 9 pounds (4kg).

As he grew up, Derrick remained so chunky that his grandmother, Carolyn Brumfield, nicknamed him Pooh, after Winnie the Pooh. Like Pooh, the boy was hefty and had a weakness for sweets. (Rose now has a tattoo, one of several, that shows a wizard holding a basketball with "Poohdini" above it to acknowledge his childhood nickname.)

Derrick first played basketball on the court of his elementary school. His basketball coach, Thomas Green, had no trouble choosing Derrick for the school's team. Green had him playing in the point guard slot.

The young athlete did not disappoint his coach and teammates. He led the Beasley squads to three straight Chicago Public League elementary titles during his sixth-, seventh-, and eighth-grade years. The budding star later recalled, "I learned a lot at Beasley. It was a special experience that helped me mature. Coach Green pushed us not only to be the best basketball player[s] we could be, but also the best person[s]."[6]

In this way, Green's influence on Derrick paid off in more ways than one. In addition to teaching him the basic skills of basketball, the coach also instilled in him the positive qualities of sportsmanship. Cyrus McGinnis, the boys' basketball coordinator for the Chicago Public League, commented, "Derrick exemplifies

*Rose's left shoulder shows his tattoo with the words "Poohdini." When Derrick was young he was nicknamed "Pooh," after Winnie the Pooh, for being a little chunky.*

# Playing for His Grandmother

**R**ose was very close to his grandmother, Carolyn Brumfield. He was devastated when she died. Derrick remembers:

> When I was ten, a phone call came at 3 A.M. My mother jumped off the bed. I got a sick feeling in my stomach, and then I saw my mom drop the phone.
>
> After my grandma died, I couldn't eat for a week. I still pray to Grandma. Every time I have a bad game, I say I'm sorry to her. She was the one who influenced me to always play hard.

Quoted in Bob Sakamoto, "2007 Mr. Basketball of Illinois," *Chicago Tribune,* March 31, 2007, p. 10.

what we have here in the Public League. He shows class and he has talent and he is the ultimate team player."[7]

## Running from the Belt

In addition to playing for Beasley, Derrick spent hours on the two-hoop court in Murray Park, a block away from the Rose family's home. Rose recalls that he played as much as he possibly could, especially on weekends and in the summer. He comments, "I had nothing to do but go out there and play basketball all day until my mother came and got me."[8]

Brenda Rose was always supportive of her son and his love of basketball. But she could also be strict with him. Rose remembers that one day he was playing inside the family's house, dribbling a ball and "shooting" into his mother's laundry basket. She warned him three times to stop, but he ignored her. At that point, Brenda came after young Derrick with a belt—the same belt that she sometimes used on his older brothers when they were disobedient.

Derrick's brothers, all of them serious hoops players, later claimed that this belt was responsible for some of their baby brother's skill on the court. They say that Derrick got his shooting ability from Reggie, his jumpers from Allan, and his ball-handling skills from Dwayne. But the credit for Derrick's speed, they say, should go to their mother. Reggie jokes, "Maybe it came from running away from that belt."[9]

## Following the Bulls

As he grew up and became more serious about basketball, Derrick had many pro athletes he could look up to as role models, but precious few who came from Englewood. One of them was Donald Whiteside, a point guard who played for Northern Illinois University and went on to a career with the Toronto Raptors and the Atlanta Hawks.

Rose recalls that watching Whiteside was inspirational to him as a young athlete. He comments, "Other than him, I really didn't have anyone else to look up to that was from my area. So in seeing him, I never gave up hope, just kept playing and then I realized that I might have a future in basketball."[10]

The young player also followed a number of basketball teams that he especially liked. His favorite, not surprisingly, was his hometown Chicago Bulls. Michael Jordan dominated not only the Bulls but also pro basketball as a whole. Indeed, in the eyes of most observers, Jordan remains the greatest player of all time.

## Playing with One Arm in a Cast

Inspired by thrilling players such as Whiteside and Jordan, Derrick continued to improve as a player. He attributes much of this improvement to his older brothers. During this period, it was mostly his next-oldest brother who helped him develop his skills, especially his willingness to hand the ball off to others if it improves the chances of successful shooting. Rose remarks, "The way I play is because of my brother Allan. Dwayne and Reggie had to work [jobs] more, so it was usually me and Allan and his friends. [When] I was 13 . . . they were 19 and 20.

*One of Derrick's role models growing up was NBA player Donald Whiteside, who also grew up in Chicago.*

When you're playing with older kids, you don't want to shoot all the time."[11]

He was especially skillful at dribbling, was amazingly fast, and had a natural ability for ambidextrous play. In part, this ability to use both hands stemmed from an accident. In the seventh grade, Derrick broke his right arm and was forced to do everything with his left hand.

His brothers used this misfortune as an opportunity. On at least one occasion, they refused to let him in the house until he made six consecutive shots with his left hand. Rose comments, "I was mad at them, because I was hungry and wanted to go in the house. But they knew what they were doing."[12]

## "Walking on Eggshells"

Derrick's brothers continued to be major influences in his life, both on and off the court. The young athlete remembers that he was always scared to do anything wicked or illegal for fear of angering them. He comments, "I was terrified of my brothers. I knew if I did something, they were going to find out. So I was just walking on eggshells throughout my whole life in Englewood."[13]

Brenda Rose also did her part to teach her son traits like personal responsibility and respect. She once told a reporter, "Derrick always has been around older people, and I'd tease him he has an old soul. But if he wasn't humble, I'd bang him on top of his head. You treat another person like you want to be treated. That stuck in his head."[14]

As part of his mother's strict outlook, Derrick had to put up with a parent who was always telling him what to do. He recalls:

She used to hate when I [didn't] make my bed in the morning. . . . She'd tell me about how irresponsible a person is that doesn't make their bed. I mean, my mom just looks at the littlest stuff . . . and it really gets to her when I don't do certain things that she wants me to do, only because she's looking out for my best interest. Like, she just wants me to be the perfect son and the perfect person.[15]

*Derrick's brothers—Allan, left, Reggie, back center, and Dwayne, right—have been a major influence in his life.*

# A "Slab of Concrete"

In addition to his school teams, Derrick played on several Amateur Athletic Union (AAU) teams, notably the Mean Streets Express. He quickly emerged as one of Chicago's best young players. He had his first public school championship in the sixth grade, and the Express was victorious in many other city-wide championships. By the time he was in eighth grade, Derrick was well known throughout Chicago, and by the time he got to Hubbard High School, he was a genuine star.

Of course, Derrick also continued to put in long hours in neighborhood pickup games at Murray Park and elsewhere. He

*Rose plays for the Mean Streets Express basketball team in July 2006.*

# "We Watch Out for Each Other"

The Rose family was not the only factor in shaping Derrick Rose's development. Brenda Rose knew that she could always count on the people in her neighborhood to help keep an eye on her son. She recalls:

> In the community he was brought up in, people around there were the babysitters. If I came home from work, I would come down the street, they'd say, You know, he's at the park. So everyone [in] the neighborhood helped out.
>
> My sons knew the changes that were in the streets. As Derrick showed more potential playing ball, they just went around and sheltered him. A lot of people don't understand, we're a close-knit family. We watch out for each other.

Quoted in Mike McGraw, "Rose Proof That Some Dreams Do Come True," *Arlington Heights (IL) Daily Herald*, July 1, 2008, p. 1.

enjoyed playing in these places despite the constant presence of drug dealers, who sometimes had to be chased away from the courts. Nonetheless, the hours that Derrick spent there paid off. Sportswriter Rick Morrissey notes, "From that slab of concrete in the middle of Englewood grew a basketball player of . . . exceptional talent."[16]

When it came to Derrick's development as an athlete during this period, Reggie was the most involved of the Rose brothers. Reggie, like his brothers, had been a standout player in high school, finishing his career as Hubbard High's all-time leading scorer. (He went on to play for the University of Idaho.) Now, as his youngest brother began to develop into a truly extraordinary player, Reggie used his own basketball skills and determination to coach Derrick.

## "Tough Love My Whole High School Career"

In addition to one-on-one training, Reggie supported his brother in other ways. For example, he coached the Mean Streets Express and built it around Derrick. Reggie always pushed this team—and his brother, of course—to find the toughest competition and confront it head-on. Derrick's older

# Watching the Bulls— or Not

June 14, 1998: Game six of the NBA championships, the Bulls versus the Jazz—the last game of Michael Jordan's career with Chicago. Rose, who was nine years old at the time, watched the game at home with family and friends.

With the Bulls trailing 86-85 and less than 30 seconds left, Jordan pulled off one of the greatest clutch performances ever. He stole the ball from forward Karl Malone at Utah's net, slowly dribbled up the court, and paused at the top of the key.

Jordan then drove inside the three-point line, faked out Jazz guard Bryon Russell, and sank a 20 foot (6m) jumper with 5.2 seconds remaining. The Jazz failed to score again, and the Bulls had their sixth championship.

But Rose missed it. As Jordan's jumper fell, Dwayne Rose changed the channel. Dwayne had done this before; he sometimes got nervous watching such crucial moments. (For some reason, no one took the remote away.)

Young Rose was in for more frustration. Joyous Chicago fans, including the older Rose brothers, were celebrating in the streets. Rose naturally wanted to join them, but he could not. He recalls, "I tried to run outside with them. They were like, 'No, go back. You're too young.'"

Quoted in Mike McGraw, "Rose Proof That Some Dreams Do Come True," *Arlington Heights (IL) Daily Herald*, July 1, 2008, p. 1.

brother applied the concept of "tough love," which stresses strict discipline as a way of instilling motivation and drive. The result, Rose later commented, was "tough love my whole high school career. . . . He just put me up against every challenge."[17]

Reggie and the other Rose brothers also continued to make sure that their kid brother stayed clear of the bad influences in their neighborhood. They were determined not to let him wreck his chances at what was starting to look likely: a career in the pros. They had seen too many failures, too many talented players who lacked the discipline and support to stay away from temptations like gang life. These temptations had cut many careers short. Rose comments, "There were a lot of people in their era that were supposed to make it and made the wrong decisions. They [Rose's brothers] didn't want me to make the same mistake."[18]

## "Raised Right"

Many observers have remarked that this strong family support has been crucial to Rose's later successes. One such commentator is another Chicago native who had an outstanding pro basketball career, Nick Anderson (now retired from the Orlando Magic). Anderson remarks, "There's a difference between being raised and brought up. He [Rose] was raised right. It carries on and off the floor. He's very respectful."[19] This attitude, in combination with his extraordinary skills, would serve the young athlete well as he started high school.

# Chapter 2

# High School

Chicago's school system lets families choose which school they would like their children to attend. When it was time for Derrick Rose to start high school, his family played an important role in this decision. The Roses wanted to find a school that stressed both a strong academic program and a strong athletic program. But they also had to consider the relative dangers of different parts of the city. Dwayne Rose comments, "When we were looking at high schools for Derrick, we looked at how many gang areas he'd have to go through to get to school."[20]

Derrick and his family chose a four-year school, Simeon Career Academy.

*Picking a high school was a difficult choice for Rose. He and his family decided on Simeon Career Academy.*

(Chicago has eleven so-called career academies, which are also sometimes called vocational-technical schools. They stress education for a variety of later college- and work-oriented experiences.) He started classes there in the fall of 2003. Simeon was (and still is) well known in the Chicago region as a powerhouse in high school sports, especially its Class AA basketball team. Its strong coaching staff and reputation for tough discipline especially appealed to Derrick.

As a freshman, Derrick was not as tall as other Simeon hoopsters, but—as everyone expected—he easily made the squad. Tim Green, one of Derrick's teammates there, recalls, "He was a little bitty guy. But he had game. That dude was good. That game Pooh has now—we called him Pooh—he had it back then. He's just had a few years to make it even better."[21]

## Honoring Benji

Simeon's basketball team was a powerhouse, but it also knew what it was like to lose a player. Small forward Ben "Benji" Wilson had led the Simeon Wolverines to their first state basketball championship. In 1984, as he entered his senior year, Benji was widely recognized as the nation's number-one high school basketball player.

But on the day before his senior season opener, Benji was shot and killed during a gang fight. The athlete had a minor argument with three gang members during his lunch break, when he was off the school grounds. According to some sources, the gang members had tried to rob him; when the athlete resisted, he was killed.

Thousands turned out to pay their respects at Benji's memorial service. The city's mayor, Harold Washington, spoke at an assembly at the school to condemn the city's skyrocketing gun violence. The mayor also promised to build a new gymnasium for Simeon and name it in Wilson's honor. This memorial gym opened in 1987.

In the years after Benji's death, the top players on the Simeon team traditionally wore his jersey number, 25. Derrick was one of them, and he wore the number all through high school. He

*Rose, in Ben Wilson Gymnasium, wears Ben's #25 on his jersey. Ben, in the portrait behind Rose, was a promising Simeon player who was shot and killed.*

commented to a reporter, "It keeps his memory alive and is a tribute to a great player."[22] Benji's brother Jeff added, "There's a spirit in him. . . . Derrick Rose has my brother's spirit."[23]

## His Freshman Year

Although he was a standout from the beginning, Derrick was not on the varsity team as a freshman. Coach Bob Hambric had a long-standing rule that freshmen could not play on varsity.

Therefore, Derrick played on the freshman-sophomore junior varsity (JV) team.

As expected, Derrick stood out for much more than just his speed and scoring abilities, although those were impressive enough. He also gained a reputation for having great court vision—the ability to see the entire court at once and react accordingly. Furthermore, he was well known for generously setting up his teammates and making sure that they stayed involved. Instead of hogging the ball and making as many points as possible himself, Derrick concentrated on seeing the team come together as a unit to win.

For his freshman year, Derrick had an excellent record. He averaged 18.5 points, 6.6 assists, 4.7 rebounds, and 2.1 steals per game. He also led the JV squad to a 24–1 record and the city championships. According to some sources, Coach Hambric bent his rule and gave Rose the chance to play on the varsity team in the state tournament, but Derrick declined even to sit on the bench. He thought that all of the varsity players deserved that honor more than he did.

## His Sophomore Year

By the start of Derrick's sophomore year in 2004, Hambric had retired. A new coach, Robert Smith, replaced him. There was no question that Rose would make the varsity squad. His debut there was a game against another Chicago powerhouse, Thornwood High.

This game was intensely anticipated by fans of high school sports. Chicago's *Sun-Times* newspaper even devoted a full page in its sports section to the event. Another measure of anticipation: the sold-out crowd bought every bit of food in the gym's concession stand even before Derrick took his first shot. They were apparently so eager to catch every minute of the game that they bought their food beforehand, so that they did not have to leave the stands.

The crowd that night included a number of college scouts and coaches who had heard about the teenage phenomenon. Already, Derrick was drawing comparisons to another young

## Simeon's Tradition

**A**mong the many honors that Simeon Career Academy has received are victories in Class AA State Boys Basketball Championships in 1984, 2006, and 2007. One of the biggest reasons for this record was the work of the school's coach, Bob Hambric. Over the course of a twenty-four-year career, Hambric became one of the most successful high school basketball coaches in Illinois history.

star, LeBron James. "King James," then in his early twenties, had signed with the NBA's Cleveland Cavaliers at the age of eighteen and became one of the league's most impressive players.

## The Varsity Debut

The crowd was not disappointed with Derrick's performance that night. He put on a spectacular show, racking up 22 points, 7 rebounds, and 5 steals. That opening game, a 53-49 victory for the Wolverines, set the pace for the rest of Simeon's season. The team ended the year with a 30-5 record. For his part, Derrick averaged 19.8 points, 5.1 rebounds, 8.3 assists, and 2.4 steals, and he shot 50 percent from the floor.

However, there were a few setbacks in this otherwise outstanding year. One came during the Pontiac Holiday Tournament, when Derrick was injured. While leaping for an inbound pass during the final minutes of a semifinal game, he suffered a sprain in his right ankle.

Nonetheless, he kept going. With three seconds on the clock and a tied score, Derrick limped to the foul line and sank one of two free throws, then fell to the ground in pain. His teammates carried him off the floor. The team made one more basket during those final seconds, and Simeon was victorious.

The outcome was different during the 2005 state championships. Chicago's Brother Rice High School defeated Simeon

77–76 in double overtime. Rose commented later that this heartbreaker was the most painful defeat of his career.

## As a Junior

Derrick's junior year season, 2005–06, ended with the Wolverines racking up a 33-4 record. Derrick, the team's star point guard, averaged 20.1 points, 5.4 rebounds, 8.7 assists, and 2.6 steals that year. He also shot 57 percent from the field.

In a season full of remarkable moments, one of the high points came during a game against Washington High School to capture the city championships. Derrick put on a 20-second performance in the third quarter that brought the house down.

With a steal and a windmill jam, the point guard rocked Chicago's United Center. (United Center is the home of the

*Rose shoots in the 2005–06 season state quarterfinals.*

# One-and-Done

In the opinion of many commentators, the NBA's "one-and-done" rule is a bad one. This rule states that to be eligible for the draft, a player must be nineteen and a year past high school graduation. Sports journalist John Feinstein is one who believes the rule is hypocritical and outdated.

In his opinion, it is unfair to force players to attend one year of college. As he argues, other high school graduates can begin their occupations without attending a university. He states:

> The silly and self-righteous people who have whined about the one-and-done rule created . . . by the NBA should quiet down. College athletes who are good enough to play on the pro level have been leaving as early as allowed for a long time now. Moses Malone [a Hall of Famer power forward/center] skipped college altogether in 1974.
>
> And, in spite of all the NCAA [National Collegiate Athletic Association] hypocrisy about "student-athletes," kids such as [forward Kevin] Love and [Derrick] Rose and many, many others are basketball players. If they really want college degrees someday, they will have the opportunity to get them.

John Feinstein, "It's One and Done, but They Still Made It Fun," *Washington Post*, April 6, 2008, p. D14.

Bulls, and it is also where high school championship games are played.) Then, with ten seconds left, he stole the ball and headed for another fast break. Forward Mario Little, bigger and stronger than Derrick, tried to contest the guard's jam. Mario's effort was in vain, however—Derrick racked up another spectacular dunk.

In the state quarterfinals that year, the Wolverines opposed Glenbrook North from Northbrook, Illinois, the defending Class AA state champions. The contest was one of the most-hyped games in state history, mostly because of the anticipated matchup between Derrick Rose and Jon Scheyer, his counter-part at Glenbrook North.

## A Championship

The Simeon squad then advanced to the Class AA state championships against Peoria's Richwoods High, held again at the United Center. Derrick scored 25 points that night and electrified the audience when, within a 20-second time span, he twice stole the ball and scored on spectacular dunks.

The end of the game was a real nail-biter. A buzzer-beater by Richwoods forced the contest into overtime. In the extra period, Derrick drained a game-winning jumper with 1.5 seconds

*Derrick Rose shoots the game-winning jumper against Peoria Richwoods. With the win, Simeon High became state champions.*

on the clock. This thrilling victory was Simeon's first state championship since 1984.

The crowd, understandably, went through the roof. After the game, the Simeon team received a police escort back into the city and enjoyed a hero's welcome on its home turf, Chicago's South Side. The school's former coach, Bob Hambric, commented that the man of the hour was clearly the team's starting point guard: "This weekend was the beginning of the legend of Derrick Rose."[24]

## "Derrick Did Us Proud"

The team finished the season 33-4, nationally ranked, and Derrick received a number of honors. Among these, he was named to the All-State Illinois team, the Electronic Arts Sports All-American second team, and the *Parade* All-American second team.

Furthermore, Derrick won praise from a number of notable commentators and others. Typical of these remarks was one that came from Nick Anderson, a standout player who spent most of his professional career with the Orlando Magic. As a high school student, Anderson had attended Simeon Career Academy, and his son Josh, a guard, played for the Wolverines alongside Derrick.

Anderson remarked on how much he appreciated Derrick's skills as well as the fact that he had come from Anderson's own hometown and alma mater. Anderson said, "I've known his family a long time, and I talk about Derrick all the time. It's good to see [talented] guys coming out of Chicago, period. But from my high school, that makes me feel good. . . . I think Derrick did us proud."[25]

## Favorite Stuff

Of course, sports dominated Derrick's life in high school. Still, his four years at Simeon were not completely about basketball. When a *USA Today* reporter asked him during his senior year about his life off the court, Derrick mentioned some of his favorite things.

He liked math, his Spanish teacher, and computers. Favorite foods were pizza, hamburgers, and ham-and-turkey sandwiches from the Potbelly chain. Television, movies, and music were also important. His dream car was a Rolls Royce Phantom. He preferred texting over e-mailing. As for his favorite athlete, that would be LeBron James.

Elsewhere, Derrick said that his favorite book was *Think Big* by Benjamin S. Carson, a pioneering African American neurosurgeon. Carson's book describes how he overcame a difficult childhood in inner-city Detroit and Boston to attend Yale University and become a pioneer in his field. The athlete comments about his hero, "When he was younger, his mother made him read every day. He became an honor-roll student in high school and then became a doctor. It made a big impression on me."[26]

## Meeting Michael Jordan

Derrick was not too busy with sports to ignore still other aspects of his life off the court. Nonetheless, his natural shyness and his focus on sports apparently kept him from spending too much time at parties and other gatherings.

This focus may have hurt his love life as well. One of Derrick's classmates, Shenikiqua Bridges, told a reporter, "If he was any other student, nobody would know him because he is so quiet. He gets a lot of attention, but he's very timid. A lot of girls would like to go out with Derrick, but I wouldn't. He's too shy."[27]

Despite this, the athlete did have a girlfriend in high school. Her name was Dana Lambert. While the two were dating, Dana's twin sister, Donna, was dating Marcus Jordan, the son of the legendary athlete Michael Jordan. Through the twins, Derrick was able to meet his hero, and he even had a chance to play in the full-size court Jordan had at home.

Rose later said that his first encounter with Air Jordan was a somewhat intimidating experience. He recalls, "The first time I met Michael, he said to me, 'What's your name?' I said, 'Derrick.' Then he smiled and said: 'I'm just playing. I know who you are.' That was pretty cool."[28]

## His Senior Year

As expected, Derrick and the Wolverines had an outstanding 2006–07 season. One of the greatest moments was a contest in January 2007 against a perennial powerhouse, number-one ranked Oak Hill Academy. (Oak Hill is a private school in Mouth of Wilson, a small town in Virginia.)

This game was played before a national television audience on ESPN. It was another squeaker—a 78-75 victory for Simeon, and Oak Hill's only loss of the year. For this game, Derrick was matched up against a formidable opponent: junior guard Brandon Jennings (who went on to join the Milwaukee Bucks in the NBA).

Despite this strong opposition, Derrick had a terrific evening: 28 points, 9 assists, and 8 rebounds. He also did well on defense, holding Jennings to zero points in the first three quarters. Derrick's thrilling performance earned him the title of *USA Today*'s national high school player of the week.

By the end of the season, Simeon had racked up a 33-2 overall record. The team was ranked first in the nation by *Sports Illustrated* magazine and sixth in *USA Today*'s national poll of high school boys' basketball.

## Another Championship

In March, the team capped things off in style with their performance at the Class AA state championships. In this title game, the Wolverines were up against the O'Fallon High School Panthers from southwestern Illinois.

The Panthers managed to contain Derrick well. He scored only 2 points, although he also had 8 assists and 7 rebounds. However, it was still a lopsided game. When the buzzer sounded, the Simeon team was victorious, 77-54. This triumph made Simeon the first school in the history of the Chicago Public League to win two consecutive state titles.

Rose has commented that the end of that game was one of the high points of his life. Not the least of his pleasure came from standing side by side with his teammates and waving at

*Rose, left, blocks the shot of an O'Fallon High player in the 2007 state championship game. Simeon won 77-54.*

the cheering crowd. Rose recalls, "It made me happy when all the others got the attention. I know I'm a part of it. I was so happy for them. They'll remember winning that game for the rest of their lives."[29]

## End-of-Season Honors

At the season's end, Derrick had amassed another remarkable record. He averaged 25.2 points, 9.1 assists, 8.8 rebounds, and 3.4 steals per game. Overall, his high school career win-loss record was a stunning 120-12.

Once again, he received a number of honors. For example, Chicago's *Tribune* newspaper awarded him its state "Mr. Basket-ball" award. Derrick shared this distinction with, among others, future NBA stars Kevin Garnett, Eddy Curry, and Shaun

*Rose participated in the 2007 McDonald's All-American game.*

Livingston. Derrick also partici-pated in the McDonald's All-Amer-ican contest, the Jordan Brand tournament, and the Nike Hoops Summit Games. He was ranked na-tionally among the top five in many polls and was chosen for the first team in *USA Today's* 2007 All-USA Team.

## "All the Showy Stuff"

Despite the honors, Derrick's mod-esty kept him from boasting in public. He was also reserved about discussing his private life. He re-flected on this during a conversation with a reporter for the *Trib-une* after winning the Mr. Basketball award. Derrick told the journalist, "Tell people that . . . I stand back from all the showy stuff and don't like all the attention on me."[30]

This interview was relatively rare. Throughout Derrick's high school career, journalists clamored for interviews. However, in general Derrick stayed away from them. His dislike of talking to the press was supported by a custom at Simeon. The team rule, with few exceptions, was no interviews.

So Derrick played his entire high school career speaking only minimally to the media, despite the fact that reporters attended his every game. This gave the athlete's fans precious little infor-mation about his life off the courts. What information they had, of course, was about his game. Sportswriter Bob Sakamoto of the *Tribune* comments, "What we knew about Derrick Rose came from watching his seamless command of a basketball game. . . . All we could know about this once-in-a-generation point guard was that he helped the Wolverines become the first Public League team to win back-to-back state championships."[31]

## College Recruitment

In the spring of 2007, Rose graduated from Simeon with a 3.2 grade point average. Meanwhile, many scouts were ranking him as the top point guard prospect in the country, so naturally several colleges intensely recruited him. Notable among these were the University of Memphis, Indiana University, DePaul University, and the University of Illinois.

Rose might have considered going straight from high school to the NBA, as LeBron James had done when he went from St. Vincent–St. Mary High School in Akron, Ohio, to the Cleveland Cavaliers. However, in 2006 the NBA had instituted a rule that anyone joining a professional team must be nineteen by the end of the calendar year of that draft, and the draft must take place at least a year after the athlete graduates from high school.

So, like several other high school phenoms, Rose headed to college—for at least a year. Once again, the entire Rose family considered the possibilities and helped Derrick make a choice. The decision-making process was kept so close within the family that the other Rose brothers did not let Derrick speak to the media until he had made his choice.

## Going to Memphis

One of the colleges most interested in signing Rose was Illinois. His home state university was especially eager to pair the point guard with another rising star, shooting guard Eric Gordon. Rose visited several colleges and seriously considered them all, but in the end he chose the University of Memphis Tigers.

The Tigers' coach, John Calipari, had been interested in the athlete for some time. Rose first caught the coach's attention when Calipari saw Rose perform in an AAU game. According to one source, the coach burst into spontaneous laughter at the sheer talent he saw.

*After considering many colleges, Rose signed with the University of Memphis. Part of his decision was being able to work with coach John Calipari, right.*

Calipari was also moved to see the athlete crying after his team lost the relatively unimportant game. The coach stated that such a strong reaction was proof of a powerful will to win: "What turned it for me was when I saw him cry after an AAU loss and the other dudes were racing to get to McDonald's. This kid was crushed by losing."[32]

## "That's Derrick"

Rose chose Memphis for several reasons. One key factor was that the school had a history of producing future NBA players. Among the Memphis alumni who went on to pro careers are Penny Hardaway, Cedric Henderson, Michael "Wild Thing" Wilson, Lorenzen Wright, Darius Washington, Shawne Williams, and Rodney Carney.

Rose was also attracted by the promise of having Rod Strickland as a mentor. At the time, Strickland, a seventeen-year NBA veteran, was Memphis's director of basketball operations.

A third important reason for choosing the Tigers was that the team had a number of proven players, and each of its starting five would be returning for Rose's freshman year. Among them were guard Chris Douglas-Roberts, nicknamed CDR, and center Joey Dorsey. Rose felt confident that they and the other veterans could teach him a lot and provide solid support during his first year of college. He commented, "For me, coming here with all these veterans to give me advice on the floor helps."[33]

Rose's future teammates reciprocated the respect. CDR commented that the rookie proved to be a good match from the beginning: "On the court, he just [fit] our offense perfectly because he can drive. He's very unselfish. Sometimes, he's a little too unselfish, I tell him. But that's Derrick."[34]

## "He Could Help Us Out"

Another of Rose's future teammates was a fellow point guard, sophomore Willie Kemp. If Rose decided to accept Memphis's

*Memphis guard Chris Douglas-Roberts defends against teammate Derrick Rose. The two players quickly became friends.*

# Getting Ready for College Ball

**R**ose first met one of his toughest opponents, Texas guard D.J. Augustin, at a summer camp in 2007 before the Chicago player started college. They took part in a twenty-minute scrimmage, during which Augustin (who was a year older) got the better of Rose and demonstrated to the in-coming college rookie just how different college ball was go-ing to be.

The matchup made Rose even more determined to suc-ceed than ever. He recalls, "After that, I knew I had to go work out. That was one of the reasons I stayed in the gym when I got back for about four hours, just working on my shooting and ballhandling, working on my layups and just running. I knew that . . . I had to get ready for college ball."

Quoted in Tim Griffin, "Rose, Augustin Battle for Spot in Final Four," ESPN.com, March 29, 2008, http://sports.espn.go.com/ncb/ncaatourney08/columns/story?id=3319718.

offer, it was likely that he would take Kemp's place in the start-ing lineup. So, before he made a decision, the potential Tiger consulted the older player.

Rose later remarked that Kemp's feelings played a major role in his decision. He wanted to avoid rivalry and make sure that Kemp would not be resentful. If Kemp had objected, Rose later stated, he would have chosen another school.

Fortunately for the Tigers, Kemp was happy to have Rose join the team. Kemp remarked, "For me, it's not about starting. I did-n't think about that one time. I just told [Derrick] he could help us out a lot if he came."[35] Rose returned the compliment when he commented, "It showed me he's a great teammate and caring."[36]

So the decision was made. Rose held a joint press conference with two teammates from Simeon who were signing with the University of Wisconsin-Milwaukee. And with that he headed to the University of Memphis.

# Chapter 3

# A Year of College

Rose was not the only high school hotshot making his college debut in 2007. Several others were expected to spark their respective teams just as powerfully. Among them were O.J. Mayo at the University of Southern California; Kevin Love at the University of California, Los Angeles (UCLA); Michael Beasley at Kansas State; Jonny Flynn at Syracuse; and Eric Gordon at Indiana.

Meanwhile, at Memphis, the media attention was almost completely on Rose, despite the presence of the other key players. Coach Calipari was not entirely comfortable with this heavy emphasis on just one team member. In his opinion, it was unfair to the other players. The coach commented, "I don't like it but it's the way things are. . . . We've got Chris Douglas-Roberts, Joey Dorsey, and yet they don't even mention their names. It's all about [Derrick]."[37]

## Chasing Greatness

Rose arrived in Memphis during the summer of 2007, before starting school. He got a running start on his training regimen, spending about four hours a day on the court. In fact, Rose worked so hard that he developed mild tendinitis in one knee and his coaches told him to ease off. He also hit the weight room, adding about fifteen pounds of muscle to his frame.

This effort also paid off in increased skill and confidence. As the team ramped up for the season, it became clear that Rose was going to dominate the team. Calipari noted that Rose's attitude had a lot to with this. The coach stated, "He's a guy who chases greatness. You have to have the habits and the work ethic to truly chase it. He does."[38] Meanwhile, Douglas-Roberts added, "He came in with so much hype—and the way he handled it—I had to admire him because he fit right in. When people say [good] things about him, he tries to put it right on us. Like, 'I've done this because of my teammates.' I admired his attitude as soon as he stepped foot on campus. There's no way you can dislike somebody like that."[39]

## "Twelve Older Brothers"

Rose had hoped to continue wearing his high school number, 25, in Memphis. But the university had retired that number in honor of its previous owner, Penny Hardaway. Instead, Rose switched to 23.

Rose was his usual reserved self as he started out the practice period around his teammates and coaches. However, he loosened up as he got to know them. Rose commented, "When I first came in, I was kind of [keeping] to myself, because I like observing people first and seeing how they are. But my team-

## The Rose Is Coming

The Tigers wanted to publicize the fact that Rose was coming to play for the team. NCAA rules, however, forbade schools from using incoming freshmen in their advertising; in turn, the university got creative.

It put up billboards around Memphis that featured a picture of a single red rose. Most of these also had an image of a returning player. Yet some signs did not even have pictures of players; instead, they simply pictured a rose with the slogan, "Witness a Rare Fall Bloom."

mates were like, 'You cannot be like that. Out of anybody on this team, you cannot be quiet.'"[40]

So the rookie worked hard to be more vocal and to gain the trust and respect of his coaches as well as his older, more experienced teammates. He disliked being labeled "just" a freshman, and felt that it should not matter how old he was. Rose commented, "If you can play, you can play."[41] (He was also careful to maintain a decent grade point average throughout the year, making sure that he would not lose his eligibility to play.)

Meanwhile, Rose's expectations about his older teammates proved accurate. Generally speaking, they helped him improve his game and feel more confident. He remarked to reporters, "They help me on and off the court. It's like having twelve older brothers."[42]

## "And That Was Just His First Game"

There was excitement in the air when the season began. For one thing, those five starters were returning, the solid backbone of a third-ranked team that had gone to a second straight National Collegiate Athletic Association (NCAA) regional final. That alone would have been enough to get fans energized, but there was now a certain highly touted freshman guard on tap as well.

Rose did not disappoint his supporters. He was the star of the show in his first collegiate game, which was against the Tennessee-Martin Skyhawks in the 2K Sports College Hoops Classic. In twenty-five minutes of play, the athlete racked up 17 points, 6 rebounds, and 5 assists as part of a lopsided 102-71 victory. He managed to score 8 out of 16 shots from the field and had four dunks, each time bringing the 16,555 cheering fans at the FedExForum to their feet. Characteristically, Rose was not satisfied with his performance, telling reporters afterward that he would only give himself a C grade.

Already, many people were wondering if Rose would follow in the footsteps of other college freshmen, such as Greg Oden and Kevin Durant, who had dominated their respective teams from day one. Douglas-Roberts, who was becoming one of Rose's closest friends and colleagues on and off the court, remarked after

*Rose, left, defends a Tennessee-Martin player in the 2K Sports College Hoops Classic. This was his first collegiate game and he scored an impressive 17 points.*

this first victory, "And that was just his first game. Imagine what he can do in a few months."[43]

## His Strengths

As the season progressed, it became clear that Rose would indeed be dominating the team. His skills and "basketball IQ" improved to match the more intense level of college ball. As they did, Rose fit more smoothly into Coach Calipari's fast-paced offense strategy, which was based on beating opponents one-on-one and attacking the basket.

Of course, not everything about Rose's play was perfect. He has always been the first to point out his deficiencies. For example, his record on the free-throw line was not outstanding. He also suffered from a relative weakness in the three-point range. He knew that working on this would become important in the NBA. He also knew that a point guard who can knock down jumpers from the three-point range is virtually impossible to guard.

# "Stop—Don't Talk About Me"

John Calipari, Rose's coach at Memphis, loved the way his star point guard played and was always surprised at how humble he was. During the year Rose spent with the Tigers, the coach remarked to a reporter after a winning game, "Do you notice when you asked about Derrick Rose to the other guys, did you see him put his head down and go, 'Oh, gee, stop—don't talk about me.' He doesn't even want us talking about him. This kid is one of the greatest teammates."

Quoted in Jeffrey Martin, "Rose, Memphis Turned into Perfect Match," McClatchy-Tribune Business News, April 7, 2008.

But Rose's assets obviously outweighed his defects. He had the speed and stamina to get anywhere on the court. This athleticism let him slip through traffic to sink shot after shot, often with a crowd-pleasing dunk. As a leader, he never slacked off, relentlessly looking for opportunities to attack. He still had his uncanny ability to see the entire court at once, and so he was able to control the tempo and direct his teammates with seeming ease. As a defender, he could get low and use his intelligence to anticipate his opponents' moves. Furthermore, he could handle big jumpers and was a brilliant clutch player.

## "Go with Whoever Is Rolling"

Perhaps most important of all was Rose's mental attitude. He was always calm on the court and never seemed to get rattled. Avoid-

*Derrick Rose's athleticism helped him make exciting shots, including crowd-pleasing dunks.*

ing arrogance, he was open about his desire to get tips from his coaches and teammates on how he could become better.

Another continuing aspect of Rose's attitude was his unselfishness. He was not afraid to make an individual play, such as driving the lane or going for a fast break, if it was the right move. However, if it was best for the team, he remained willing to share the ball rather than score himself. Rose's friend CDR commented, "It's fine with this team to go with whoever is rolling, and if he's rolling he better [take the shots]. And if he doesn't, I'll be on him to do it."[44]

Because of his skills and size—he is big for a point guard—Rose was often compared to another gifted point guard, 6 foot 4 inch (1.95m) Jason Kidd. One person who made this comparison was Calipari. The coach commented, "His [Rose's] speed, athleticism and jumping ability put him in the upper echelon [level] of all basketball, not just college basketball. In terms of reaction, seeing things before they happen, and making a play before others even know what's going on, that's where [Rose and Kidd are] alike."[45]

## The Season

Rose was getting most of the attention paid that year to the Tigers. However, he was by no means the team's only strong player. Perhaps most crucial—to the team as a whole and to Rose's performance—was Douglas-Roberts.

Working together, they had developed into an unstoppable duo. Calipari's counterpart at Kansas, Bill Self, reflected on the duo's danger when he remarked on the importance of shutting them down. He commented, "We have to eliminate them getting to the paint. When they get to the paint, good things [for Memphis] generally happen."[46]

The Rose-CDR duo was one important element in helping the team rack up an astounding 26-0 start to the season. This record skyrocketed the team from their number-three ranking to the number-one spot for the first time in more than twenty-five years. In fact, the Tigers did not suffer their first loss of the season until February 2008, falling to the University of Tennessee Volunteers, 66-62.

*Rose shoots against the Tennessee Volunteers in February 2008. The Memphis Tigers suffered their first loss of the season in this game.*

## Speaking Out

In the wake of this crushing defeat, discouraged veterans like Douglas-Roberts and Dorsey hid their disappointment by retreating to the locker room and then quickly leaving the stadium. But not Rose. He faced the failure head-on and was one of only a few Tigers who agreed to talk to the media. He did not deny his disappointment, but he also promised that he would not let it sink him into despair. Reporter Dan Wolken comments, "When they lost to Tennessee, their first loss of the season, every veteran guy was back in the locker room with their jersey over their face. Derrick was the one who came out and spoke first. I have a lot of respect for him for doing that. . . . He was very deferential, almost unaware that he is a superstar."[47]

## "A Pretty Agreeable Kid"

**D**an Wolken, a sportswriter for Memphis's *Commercial Appeal* newspaper, is typical of the many commentators who have been impressed with Rose's unshowy attitude, especially compared with other top athletes. In Wolken's opinion, Rose is natural and unpretentious because his family protected him from negative influences. The writer comments:

> Derrick's a pretty agreeable kid. I almost want to say he doesn't know any better. . . . Some other guys, they're more polished . . . and almost have this hard edge, a phoniness. Derrick was sheltered, so he still has that innocence to him and it's real.

> My sense is that he didn't understand what he was, what he is. I never got the sense he understood what a freak [of athletic ability] he is. That might change. . . . I hope it doesn't change, because it's very endearing.

Quoted in Teddy Greenstein, "Rose, Beasley Still Just Kids; Writers Share Views of Draft Prospects," *Chicago Tribune*, June 24, 2008, p.3.

The loss to Tennessee proved to be the only one the Tigers suffered that year. After winning 102 games in the current and two preceding seasons, the Tigers tied the NCAA second-highest win total in a three-year period in Division I history nearly matching the previous record (104) set by the University of Kentucky's Wildcats from 1994 to 1996. (Later, after Rose had moved on, Memphis did tie Kentucky's record.)

## On to the Big Dance

As the season's end drew near, Rose increasingly focused on working the defense, hoping to shut down such tough players as Texas's D.J. Augustin and UCLA's Darren Collison. Rose ended the regular season with an average of 14.9 points, 4.7 assists, 4.5 rebounds, and 1.2 steals. He also made 48 percent of his shots from the floor. This performance earned the athlete All-American Third Team honors, and he placed as a finalist for both the Bob Cousy and John R. Wooden awards.

Meanwhile, the Memphis team's winning streak just kept going. The Tigers captured the Conference USA Tournament and ended the regular season with a 33-1 record, 38-2 overall. The team was the number-one seed in the South Region and easily made its way to the 2008 Final Four.

Rose, naturally, was crucial to this advance, though he remained modest and seemed grateful just for the chances he had. He told a reporter, "I've been through a lot just growing up like I did, poor and everything. Just to be here, getting a scholarship, playing college basketball and for my first year to be in the Final Four, it all means a lot."[48]

## The Championship Game

The next stop for the Tigers was the NCAA championship game. It pitted the team against the University of Kansas Jayhawks. The contest took place at the Alamodome in San Antonio, Texas.

Rose was slow off the mark that evening. In the first half, he attempted only four shots. The half was quiet overall, with nei-

*Rose looks for room to shoot against Kansas' Darnell Jackson in the NCAA championship game in April 2008. It was a hard fought game that Memphis lost 75-68.*

ther team making any outstanding moves. At halftime, the Tigers trailed 33-28.

Later in the contest, though, Rose exploded, taking control of the game despite having to play on a twisted ankle. He scored 14 points in one rush midway through the half, capping the run by taking an inbound pass with the shot clock about to expire. He then hit a jumper that bounced off the glass and fell at the buzzer, giving the Tigers a seven-point lead.

Although the Tigers' lead slipped, time was running out fast and it looked like the championship was assured. Then things took another twist. With 10.8 seconds left in regulation play and the Tigers up by only two, Rose was fouled and given two free throws. On the bench, Calipari—no doubt along with every other Tigers fan—was praying. The coach later recalled, "I said, 'Lord, if he makes this, these two, we're supposed to be national champs. And if that's your will, I'm fine. And if he misses them, and we're not, I'm fine with that, too.' That's what I said in my mind. I'm probably not supposed to say that, religiously, but that's what it was."[49]

# A Heartbreaker

It was not to be. Rose missed the first of his free throws, with the ball bouncing in and out of the hoop. This was too much like the Tigers' performance earlier in the year, when the team as a whole had performed poorly at the free-throw line. Most of the time this did not matter much because the rest of their play was so strong. This time, it did matter.

Rose sank his second basket, but nonetheless the Tigers now had only a razor-thin three-point lead. Rose's bad luck at the free-throw line gave the Jayhawks point guard, Mario Chalmers, the opportunity to hit a three-pointer with a mere 2.1 seconds left in the game. Then, after the contest went into overtime, the fortunes of the two teams reversed. The Jayhawks made steady gains; when the final buzzer sounded, the Kansas team was victorious, 75-68.

Rose scored 17 points during the game, grabbed 6 rebounds, and had 7 assists. For the overall tournament, he averaged 20.8 points, 6.5 rebounds, and 6 assists. The rest of the team performed at their highest level as well, but it had not been enough. Afterward, the point guard who hated to lose had trouble controlling his emotions. Outside Memphis's locker room, Rose cried and hugged supporters, including his brother Reggie and his spiritual adviser, the Reverend Jesse Jackson. (Jackson has been an important factor in sustaining Rose's deep religious faith. The athlete has often remarked that he credits his skills and good fortune to his Christian beliefs.)

# Declaring for the NBA

The heartbreak of this near-championship notwithstanding, Rose was still one of the top college players in the country— perhaps *the* top. By this time, there was widespread speculation that he would choose to skip the rest of his time in college. Rose was just one of many players for whom the temptation is strong

*Former Chicago Bulls point guard B.J. Armstrong, seen here, became Rose's agent before the NBA draft and helped keep Rose focused.*

to do the minimum amount of studying needed to stay in school for a year. They can then jump to the serious money in the NBA. Since he was now the right age and a year out of high school, he was eligible to turn pro.

And that is exactly what the athlete decided to do. On April 15 he announced that he would declare for the draft. In his official statement, Rose said, "I have decided to make myself eligible for the 2008 NBA Draft. This is not a step I take lightly, although it has always been a dream of mine to play in the NBA. After weighing all of the options . . . I feel that it is the right time for me to take this step."[50]

## Preparing for the Draft

Rose has commented that his year at the University of Memphis was a blessing, particularly because the discipline fostered by John Calipari helped him improve his strength and learn the subtleties of the game. He says, "My only regret is not winning a national title for the University of Memphis. I am, however, very excited about the prospect of playing in the NBA and continuing to strive to be the best player and the best person I can be."[51]

In the period leading up to the draft, Rose worked hard to stay in shape. His agent, former Bulls point guard B.J. Armstrong, made sure he stayed focused. One way Armstrong did this was to have his client work out in Los Angeles, not in his hometown. This helped the athlete concentrate on basketball, not on friends or other distractions.

During this time, representatives from the Chicago Bulls and the Miami Heat—the two teams that were most interested in him—watched Rose work out. Now, it was up to them and the other pro teams to decide the next step in Rose's dazzling career.

# Chapter 4

# NBA Rookie Year

**N**aturally, Rose was excited about the upcoming draft. For months, he had told reporters that it did not matter too much what team he was going to—he would be happy just to be in the NBA.

However, as the time grew closer he admitted to reporters that he really wanted to play for his hometown team. Becoming a Bull, Rose said, would be a dream come true. He joked, "I'll probably faint if they call my name, I'll need a paramedic close by."[52]

## "Get Ready! Today Is Your Day!"

For a long time, that seemed like a remote possibility. When Rose first told his agent that he wanted to start his professional career in Chicago, they both laughed. This was because, before the draft, Chicago had only a 1.7 percent chance of landing the top pick. (The draft is for the teams that did not make the play-offs in the previous season, and it is weighted to give the teams with the worst records the best chance of getting the first picks.)

In a surprise twist, however, the Bulls beat the odds and snagged the first pick. Many observers thought that Chicago would use it to choose another highly touted player, forward Michael Beasley of Kansas State.

Beasley and Rose were friends and admired each other's abilities. In fact, at a joint press conference, Rose stated that Beasley was the best choice. Laughing, Beasley repaid the compliment,

*Rose, left, and Michael Beasley, right, were both possible draft picks for the Chicago Bulls.*

pointing out that it was Rose, not himself, who had led his team to a national championship game.

The day of the draft was June 26, 2008. Rose was in New York City for the big event. His day started at 11:00 A.M. at his hotel with a phone call from his best friend since childhood, Randall Hampton. The athlete heard some loud music, followed by Hampton yelling, "Get ready! Today is your day!"[53]

That evening, at the ceremony where the choices were announced, the news was what Rose had hoped for. Most commentators predicted that he would be headed to Miami. Instead, his hometown team used its first overall pick to choose him.

## "Kind of Crazy"

Rose managed to avoid fainting when the news was announced. Instead, grinning the whole time, he stood up, put on a red Bulls cap, hugged his family and friends, and shook hands with Beasley. He then mounted the stage and, with a shy smile, posed for the cameras with NBA commissioner David Stern. Rose commented to the audience, "I played this moment over and over in my mind a thousand times, and this is as good as it gets. I will represent my family, the city of Chicago and the Chicago Bulls to the best of my ability."[54]

# No Knuckleheads

In a number of interviews, Rose has expressed appreciation for his fellow Bulls. He says that he is very happy that they generally have a positive attitude. The following is typical of his comments:

> The one thing I love about our team is we have good characters. We have good players, no character-issue guys who are going to get in trouble a lot, we've got some good solid veterans and we've got some weapons on our team. Two years ago we were the No.1 offense in the NBA. . . .

> I'm blessed that [we] don't have anyone on our team that's hardheaded or is a knucklehead. They're all good guys. Not that I'll ever be a knucklehead, but this year has made me feel much older. Playing all of these games, getting to know everything about the NBA, you realize that you are your own business. You have business meetings to go to, signings to go to. Like I'm only 20, but the stuff I'm doing the average 20-year-old isn't doing.

Quoted in Scoop Jackson, "The Rose That Rose from Concrete," ESPN.com, April 15, 2009. http://sports.espn.go.com/chicago/columns/story?columnist=jackson_scoop&id=4070218.

*Rose shakes hands with NBA commissioner David Stern at the 2008 NBA draft. The Chicago Bulls selected Derrick Rose as the first overall pick.*

Chicago's choice made history. Rose was only the second guard to be taken as a number-one pick overall since the Los Angeles Lakers opted for Magic Johnson in 1979. (The other was Allen Iverson, chosen by the Philadelphia 76ers in 1996.) Furthermore, Rose was the first former Chicago Public League player in twenty-seven years to be the first pick by any pro team.

The event also marked the first time that the first three picks were college freshmen. The others were Michael Beasley to Miami and O.J. Mayo to Minnesota. The three young men knew each other well, and for years they had half-jokingly talked about being drafted together. Beasley commented, "We all grew up . . . playing against each other and we all made a pact together that we would all be here. Just to see it all fall into place and see it all happen is kind of crazy."[55]

## "It Makes You Proud"

Meanwhile, plenty of other people were celebrating as well. In their offices, members of the Bulls organization cheered as their choice became public. In Chicago's Murray Park, where Rose had played as a boy, a large crowd roared when Stern made his announcement. One of the celebrants, Rose's childhood friend Ephraim Brantley, commented, "Everybody knows Derrick. And even though he is the talk of the town tonight, he is still one of us. We all know a lot of bad things have happened in our neighborhood. But Derrick being drafted Number One kind of lifts everybody up. It makes you proud to be from Englewood."[56] Rose's elementary school, Beasley Academic Center, also celebrated. The school's basketball coach, Thomas Green, commented, "Everyone from the engineering department to the teachers [is] just so proud of him. Elementary school teachers have so much impact on a person's life and we at Beasley feel we had a good influence on Derrick. This is where it all started for him and we all feel great."[57]

## Turning the Bulls Around

Naturally, Rose's skills on the court were the primary reason he was chosen. But the Bulls' choice was also influenced by the nature of how the NBA game was changing. For years, inside scorer-rebounders had been generally preferred over point guards.

However, recent trends in league play emphasizing the importance of perimeter players and up-tempo running attacks that the point guard directs, were making Rose's position increasingly important. Furthermore, Rose was expected to fit in well with the style favored by Vinny Del Negro, the team's new coach. Del Negro liked an up-tempo offense and pick-and-rolls, both of which require a topnotch point guard.

*Rose, left, worked well with new Chicago Bulls coach Vinny Del Negro, right.*

Perhaps most important of all was Rose's confidence in himself as a team leader. Chicago had ruled the pro basketball world for years during the Michael Jordan era. More recently, however, it had suffered a number of setbacks, including the firing of Del Negro's predecessors, Scott Skiles and Jim Boylan, after their dismal 33-49 season.

## Taking It Slow

Since the Bulls needed steady, inspirational guidance on the court, the team's new pick was seen as someone who could boost morale and unify the team. In addition to Rose, Chicago also now had a promising new coach and a number of strong returning players. The Bulls were poised to become a powerful force again.

For all of these reasons, Rose fit in well with the team's long-range plan. Part of that plan was to let Rose develop slowly. The Bulls organization understood that even the best players need to take their time. For example, the player Rose has been most often compared with, Jason Kidd, did not have a winning NBA season until his fourth year.

Many observers and analysts applauded the Bulls' decision to develop Rose slowly. ESPN commentator Jay Bilas stated, "For the long term, I think Rose is the best prospect. . . . When you can get a great point guard, I think you pull the trigger on it."[58]

## Summer

In the meantime, there was plenty to do. Rose was part of the USA Select Team, which helped train the national team for the upcoming Beijing Olympics. Going toe to toe against these veterans, Rose later commented, was great preparation for his fast-approaching pro debut. The point guard also participated in the Bulls' minicamp and practice sessions in suburban Deerfield, Illinois.

Furthermore, in anticipation of the season, Coach Del Negro gave Rose a questionnaire to complete after every game. Its questions included: What offensive sets worked well against this team? What defensive sets were they in? Who did you guard? Was he a post-up player, getting into position in the low post under the basket below the foul line? What was effective and what was not? What did you learn about this team, and what did you learn in transition? Thinking about these questions helped Rose analyze specific opponents and find ways to neutralize them. He also had plenty of his own questions during the preseason. He recalled, "I asked a lot. . . . I lost count. [But] I felt very comfortable out there.

I can't wait to get down to Orlando [for a Pro Summer League game] and start playing."[59]

Rose played two games in this tournament until a minor case of tendinitis in his right knee forced him to the sidelines. He had another reason for not pushing himself too much during the months before the season started. Knowing that the really hard work would come soon, he spent much of his time resting and relaxing with pastimes like movies and video games. One particular pleasure during this period involved another sport: He threw out the first pitch at a Chicago Cubs–Chicago White Sox game.

*Rose throws out the first pitch before a Chicago Cubs–Chicago White Sox game in June 2008.*

# "A Quiet Leader"

Just as Rose has been full of praise about his teammates on the Bulls, they have returned the compliments. One such player is Ben Gordon, who was so effective working with Rose. Answering criticism that the point guard is not vocal enough on the court, Gordon commented, "Derrick has always been a quiet leader anyway. I watched him a handful of times when he was in high school and he never said a word out there. He just kind of led with his play and he just has this presence where he doesn't have to say much. . . . But when he needs to speak, step up and be vocal, he does."

Quoted in Mike Dodd, "Rose Blossoms," *USA Today*, December 16, 2008, p. C1.

## "I Love the Big Stage"

Meanwhile, Rose became rich. He signed a two-year contract with the Bulls for about $10 million, with a team option of over $5.5 million for a third season. It was quite a homecoming present for a kid from the tough Chicago streets who had grown up with the Bulls. He told a reporter, "It means a lot to play at home. They had great players like Michael Jordan, Scottie Pippen, Dennis Rodman. . . . Just knowing that I can be a part of that history, it's amazing."[60]

Before the season began, reporters often asked Rose if he was worried about playing in his hometown. They wondered if he was concerned about pressures and distractions. The athlete replied that he had played in Chicago for years with intense attention paid to him, so it was not new. After all, Rose pointed out, he had already played in the Bulls' home, United Center. He commented, "It was a big stage. I love the big stage."[61]

Rose also said that the main downside he could see to playing in his hometown was that people would be constantly asking him to get them free tickets and do other favors. Everything else, he thought, would be positive. He remarked, "I get to see my family, I get to see my friends, and I'm not homesick."[62]

## The Big Night

Wearing his Bulls jersey—number 1—for the first time in public games, Rose played in all eight games of the preseason. It quickly became clear that he would be a starter for the first game of the regular season. For the occasion—the October 28, 2008, matchup against the Milwaukee Bucks—the Rose family and their friends were out in force, in a suite Rose had rented. When the Bulls announcer boomed that one of the players was from Chicago, Rose's group—and the rest of the crowd—roared their approval. It was so loud, Dwayne Rose recalls, that he could not hear his brother's name called out.

The game was especially sweet because it was a victory for the Bulls, 108-95. While his teammates Luol Deng and Ben Gordon were the Bulls' big scorers of the evening, the rookie performed well. Rose barely missed a double-double, and he

## Taking the Ball from Day One

In this interview excerpt, Bulls Vice President of Basketball Operations John Paxson comments on some of his star point guard's best qualities:

> People don't realize how difficult the point guard position is in our league and how you have to run a team, take control, lead and get everybody involved. For Derrick to take the ball from Day One and lead us and play at the level he played at is really, really difficult.
>
> Plus, he's one of the finest young men I've been around. He has humility. He wants to be a great player. He goes about his business as a professional should. Beyond his wonderful basketball talent, his personality is something we're very fortunate to have.

Quoted in K.C. Johnson, "The Prize Is Right," *Chicago Tribune*, April 23, 2009.

*Rose playing in his first NBA game on October 28, 2008. The Bulls won 108-95, and Rose played a solid game with good stats.*

finished the contest with 11 points, 4 rebounds, 4 turnovers, 3 steals, and 9 assists in just over thirty-two minutes of play. (A double-double is when a player achieves a double-digit number in two of three categories: points, rebounds, assists, steals, and blocked shots.)

Afterward, Rose insisted that while on the court he was barely aware that he was making his big-time debut. The athlete commented, "I wasn't really thinking about it being my first game as a Bull. I was out there trying to win. That's the main thing that was on my mind."[63]

## The Season Continues

Rose continued to electrify fans as the season progressed. He was plagued early on by nagging injuries, from a strained right hip to back spasms. But he quietly gutted it out, becoming the first Bulls draftee since Michael Jordan to score ten points or more in each of his first ten games. He also earned Eastern Conference Rookie of the Month honors in both November and December.

Typical of this strong early performance was a November game against the Philadelphia 76ers. A good example of the moves he made during this contest came when he caught fast-breaking guard Andre Miller from behind; as Miller went for a layup, Rose swatted the ball across the sideline. Another was during the Bulls' final possession of the first half. Rose used a crossover dribble to leave Miller far behind, and he was credited with a basket when center Samuel Dalembert goal-tended his shot.

By the end of the game, which was a 103-92 win for the Bulls, Rose had racked up 18 points and 10 assists. The occasion also marked the second double-double of his career, the first with points and assists. (His first double-double had been earlier in November, in a close home loss to the Atlanta Hawks.)

## Back to Memphis

In December, the Bulls traveled to Memphis to face the Grizzlies—a homecoming of sorts for the former college star. Before the game, Rose remarked to reporters that he would be playing in front of many friends and former teammates. He joked, "I'm going to need a lot of tickets. I don't know how many yet, but it's going to be a lot."[64]

He added that he was very grateful for his year in Memphis. He had gained a lot from his experience there, he said, and had needed that year to prepare for the high-pressure world of the NBA. He also credited his former college coach, John Calipari, with much of his success, commenting that they still spoke weekly: "I can talk to Coach Cal about anything—family, girls. That's the type of person he is. He's a helpful guy. I look at him like a father figure. I used to go to his house a lot and he would help me with so much."[65] Disappointingly, the Bulls lost that matchup, 103-96. Still, Rose had a solid game, scoring 12 points and making 11 assists. As they had for some time, he and shooting guard Ben Gordon, who was the night's high scorer, made an especially effective team.

In a home game the following month, Chicago got its revenge by beating the Grizzlies 96-86. Rose finished that game with 26 points and 3 assists, with especially impressive jump shots and drives to the basket.

## A Dangerous Apple

Rose continued to be plagued by injuries, though not seriously. In November, for example, he sat out a practice to rest back muscles that had started spasming. Then, in December, he injured his right hip flexor, left the court, and did not return. Later, he said that he felt he could have come back into the game, but his coaches still had him sit it out.

Rose had another injury in December, but this one was off the court. He was forced to miss a practice after slicing his arm. The accident, which needed ten stitches, happened when he rolled onto a knife while eating an apple in bed. Rose remarked, "It was a silly incident. I was cutting up some food and . . . getting lazy in bed. I went to go get a bottle of water, came back, forgot the knife was there, then sat down and sliced my arm. I panicked when it first happened and called my trainer. It was painful but I should be alright."[66] Needless to say, the rookie was teased by his teammates over the accident. Guard Larry Hughes commented, "Mama always said don't eat in bed, right? We'll make fun of him a little bit."[67]

## The Playoffs Begin

The season continued to be a strong one for Rose. In February, he took part in the NBA's All-Star Weekend. During that tournament's

Rookie Challenge, he scored four points and led the rookies with seven assists. Rose also became the first rookie to claim the trophy in the weekend's Skills Challenge.

Rose suffered from a brief midseason slump, but he sprang back and won the Eastern Conference Rookie of the Month honors again in March. The guard finished the year on a high note, averaging 16.8 points, 6.3 assists, and 3.9 rebounds per game, making 47.5 percent of his shots from the two-point range.

The team as a whole clearly benefited from the presence of Rose and several other new players, notably forward John

*Rose became the first rookie to win the Skills Challenge at the NBA All-Star Weekend in 2009.*

Salmons and 7 foot (2.1m) center Brad Miller. The Bulls finished the regular season 12–4, qualifying them for the seventh seed in the Eastern Conference.

The team now faced the Boston Celtics, the league's defending champions. The first of the seven playoff games in the series took place on April 18 at TD Garden, Boston's home court.

In his pro playoff debut, televised to a massive national audience, Rose put on a terrific show. He scored a blazing 36 points—a game high and a career high—on 63 percent shooting. This tied the record for rookie scoring in a debut playoff set in 1970 by Milwaukee's Lew Alcindor (later known as Kareem Abdul-Jabbar).

In his forty-nine minutes of play, Rose also racked up 11 assists and 4 rebounds, sank all 12 free-throw attempts, and added a steal for good measure. When the game ended, in overtime, the Bulls were victorious, 105-103. It was the first time the Bulls had ever beaten the Celtics in a postseason game.

## "Wait a Second"

Rose disappeared from public view the next day, saying that he needed distance from well-meaning friends wanting to congratulate him. The athlete spent most of that time watching DVDs and quietly relaxing to maintain his focus on the game. He commented, "People were calling me and texting me, but I really didn't get into it. I don't have my phone on loud when I'm watching my movies. I missed a lot of calls. But they know I'm here [in Boston] for business."[68]

Rose succeeded in staying focused. In the rest of the series, he pulled off some moves that stunned even seasoned observers of the game. One of the most remarkable of these came during the second game. With about eight minutes remaining, Rose set out to foil a modified fast break. Instead of trying to beat Rose off the dribble, Celtics small forward/shooting guard Paul Pierce lobbed a pass to his teammate Eddie House in the corner. Rose was backpedaling but sensed the pass. He whirled around on the foul line, took two enormous strides, closed out on House's three-pointer, and tipped the shot. Writer Bill Simmons comments,

"Watching it live, I rewound the play on TiVo even though the game was still going—just for the record, I never, ever, ever rewind plays until the commercial—and only because I was thinking, 'Wait a second, he didn't just take two steps from the foul line and block a corner three, did he?' Yup. He did."[69]

## Not the Best of Seven for Chicago

The series was a nail-biter until the end, with every game going into overtime, and Rose provided his share of the excitement. For example, his block of a shot by guard Rajon Rondo during the final seconds of triple overtime in game six helped force a seventh game. Rose maintained his strong pace throughout the playoffs, averaging 19.7 points, with 6.4 assists and 6.3 rebounds for the tournament.

When the tournament ended, however, the Celtics prevailed, and Rose's dream of going to the championships as a rookie disappeared. Nonetheless, he had had an outstanding year, starting strong and never really slowing. His overall performance was honored when Rose was named the NBA's Rookie of the Year, joining fellow Bulls Michael Jordan (1985) and Elton Brand (2000) in receiving that honor.

At the end of the season, a reporter asked Rose what his best and worst moments had been. The guard modestly answered that his best moment was an overtime victory over the Clippers in December that was decided by Ben Gordon's four-point play. (When he was fouled while making a three-point shot and then made the free throw.) As for his worst moment, Rose noted the Bulls' five-game losing streak in January, which had been terrible because he was unaccustomed to losing.

## Summer 2009

In the off-season of 2009, Rose organized his first youth basketball camp, which was held in Deerfield, where the Bulls worked out. Rose remarked that he enjoyed the event: "It's [great] trying to get kids out here to teach them the fundamentals of basketball, to have fun and compete. . . . There are some good players out there."[70]

*Rose holds up his trophy on April 23, 2009, after winning the NBA Rookie of the Year Award.*

The athlete also journeyed to the Team USA minicamp in Las Vegas. He was hoping to land a spot on the team that will represent the United States in the world championships in Turkey in 2010 and the 2012 Olympics in London. (As of February 2010, Rose was on the preliminary roster—along with his idol LeBron James.)

Rose spent most of his time in the Bulls' gym, working in particular on his jump shot. He also worked out in Santa Monica,

*Rose practices during minicamp for the USA men's basketball team. Rose hopes to play with the team in the 2012 Olympics in London.*

California, with his personal trainer, Rob McClanaghan, who had been a walk-on guard at Syracuse. As before, Rose chose to train in California to avoid distractions. He comments, "Other than working out, going to the movies, I was in the house the whole time."[71]

## Another Contender

During Rose's rookie season, another contest and another of Chicago's favorite sons had also captured the public eye: the presidential campaign of Illinois senator Barack Obama. It was no secret that Obama, a hoops fanatic, was a huge fan of the athlete. The presidential candidate frequently remarked that he was proud that Rose was from Chicago. He said, "I think Derrick Rose is the man. He's Jason Kidd with a jump shot."[72] The athlete was surprised and pleased to be noticed by such a famous figure. When he was told about Obama's comment, Rose replied, "Wow, that's big. Someone running for president already comparing me to a veteran. I can't let that get to my head. I still have to get out there and play."[73]

## Meeting the First Fan

In February 2009 the Bulls were in Washington, D.C., for a game against the Wizards. Obama—now the commander in chief—attended the contest (which the Bulls lost, 113-90). The Chicago team was later invited to the White House, an experience that Rose said was one of the great moments of his life. He comments:

> Usually, you're nervous around a person of his stature and power, but he made us feel at ease. He was like one of the guys. He was laughing and joking with us and knew everybody on the team by name.

> We toured the White House and took pictures with the president. [Assistant coach] Pete Myers gave me a copy of [Obama's] book and he autographed it for me.[74]

President Obama put the team at ease by joking with them during the photo session. He commented that he wanted to stand next to shooting guard Ben Gordon, because Gordon was not as tall as the others. (Actually, Gordon is 6 feet 3 inches [1.8m], the same as Rose; Obama is two inches shorter).

The meeting at the White House was one of the most exciting moments in a remarkable year for the athlete. Now it was time to look to the future.

# Chapter 5

# The Future

**O**f course, no one can predict exactly what the future will bring for Derrick Rose. He is still very young, and there are no guarantees of anything in the fast-changing world of pro sports.

Nonetheless, the many fans, journalists, and commentators following Rose's dazzling career continue to make guesses—reasonable ones, for the most part—about where his life and career might lead. Most of them agree that, if Rose can avoid injury and the kinds of problems that have plagued some other athletes, there are few limits on what he could accomplish. Writer Bill Simmons comments, "The ceiling has been removed for Rose. I am prepared for anything over the next 12 years. Anything."[75]

## Room for Improvement

Naturally, much of the speculation about the athlete's future revolves around his skills on the court. Rose is extravagantly gifted. He continues to be blindingly fast, so strong that he often overpowers opponents, with great instincts and court vision. He also remains an unselfish, focused leader—the kind of player whose presence makes his teammates perform better as well.

However, even the most gifted athletes always have room for improvement, and Rose is no exception. While acknowledging

Rose's strengths, many observers also point out his weak spots. For example, they say, he needs to be more vocal and aggressive on the court. Some observers also hope that he can develop a more consistent jumper and improve his three-pointers.

Still another area where he could get even better is in his ability to change speeds quickly. The speed of NBA play is highly variable—sometimes faster than college ball and sometimes slower. Rose usually sets his speed at fast—very fast—and generally this is a good thing. However, those watching him hope that in time he will become more adept at changing gears because there are many occasions during the course of a game in which offensive play can be helped by slowing the tempo.

All of these shortcomings, of course, can be fixed. Rose's ability to improve dramatically in the years to come seems assured. His penchant for hard work, his willingness to hear constructive criticism, and his self-motivation and accurate self-criticism all speak well for the future. The athlete comments, "I need to work on everything. All-around game. My mental approach to the game. Dribbling. Passing. Jump shot. Learning about my opponent. It's a lot of things."[76]

## Living Right

For all athletes, the long hours of training—on the court and in the weight room, on the field or around the running track—are only part of what is needed to maintain and improve their abilities. Some of the other aspects of an athlete's life are also physical, such as eating right. Others are mental disciplines, such as staying focused and avoiding distractions that could ruin a single game or an entire career.

For Rose, one important part of his physical training will be to learn to improve his diet. He is still barely out of his teen years, and like many his age he has bad eating habits. Even serious athletes often do not realize until they are older that a healthy diet and lifestyle translate into improved stamina and performance.

Rose is as guilty of this as any other young person. In particular, he is famous for his fondness for sweets. The athlete has had a his-

*Rose practices hard and puts in long hours of training to improve his abilities.*

tory of suffering from upset stomachs, which may simply be caused by eating so much candy—a habit his teammates have always teased him about. His fellow player at Memphis, Chris Douglas-Roberts, once remarked, "He eats Gummy Bears and Starbursts for breakfast, and Twizzlers and Honey Buns for dinner. That's why his stomach hurts. We tell Derrick the whole year, 'Stop eating so many Gummy Bears and Sour Straws.' But he can't."[77]

## On the Road

However, as he gets older and becomes more experienced, this will no doubt change. Especially during the season, Rose works closely with a nutritionist to make sure he has a healthy diet.

Related to this, of course, is the need for proper rest. When the team goes on the road, Rose's family members, and sometimes his friend Randall Hampton, often travel with him. Part of their job, on the road or at home, is to ensure that Rose gets enough rest and good nutrition. (At home, of course, he also has the rest of the family to make sure he maintains his health.)

Adjustments in his lifestyle—particularly eating and sleeping habits—were especially difficult for Rose when he started traveling with the Bulls. For example, he was in the new house he bought for himself only a few days before the team took its first road trip. The athlete recalls,

> I was just getting used to my bed, and then like two days after that, we have to leave for the trip. So I wasn't getting a full night of sleep because I wasn't used to the beds. Like everything changes. I don't think I was eating right. But my brothers, they helped me out by taking me out for something. If they didn't, I'd be in the room eating room service all day.[78]

## Ben Gordon Leaves

Of course, many of the potential problems Rose faces in his new life will decline as he becomes more accustomed to its stressors. Many of these potential problems will not be issues at all if he can control them. However, he will not be able to control some factors.

For example, in the summer of 2009 something happened to change the course of events for Rose and the Bulls. The team's most prolific scorer, Ben Gordon, announced that he was leaving Chicago. He moved to the Detroit Pistons, signing a five-year contract worth more than $50 million.

Gordon had been an important part of Rose's success as a Bull. The two had worked closely in the Bulls' backcourt, generally with the older player on the perimeter, ready to shoot. Together, they had been an important part of the team's effectiveness.

Gordon's departure created a big hole alongside Rose, one that was not easy to fill. Without the shooting guard, Rose will have to shoulder more of the burden of leading the team. Furthermore, Gordon had a reputation as someone who could be relied on to score late in the game—a role that Rose will have to help fulfill.

*Rose, left, lost his best scoring partner when Ben Gordon, right, decided to leave the Bulls and play for the Detroit Pistons.*

## "I'm Gonna Miss Him a Lot"

Without Gordon, Rose would have a more difficult time maintaining his own spectacular numbers and setting new records. In his first season without Gordon Rose's numbers did fall off—however, only slightly. By November of the 2009–10 season, Rose was averaging 15.4 points a game versus the 2008–09 season when he averaged 16.8 points a game. ESPN.com commentator Kevin Arnovitz has noted that, if Rose does falter, it may not be caused by his own deficiencies. Arnovitz remarks, "Even a magician needs props, and Rose lost his best aide in Gordon. It's possible Rose could endure a very rough [near future] with the Bulls. If he does, it might say a lot more about his team's roster than it does any lack of resolve on Rose's part."[79]

The point guard himself has clearly been concerned about the challenges that Gordon's departure has created. He has noted that Gordon's presence will be greatly missed. Acknowledging that the shooting guard had made a financial choice to switch teams, Rose commented to a reporter, "Ben is a great player, one of the best scorers I've ever played with, a great guy. He had to make a business move going to Detroit. . . . I'm gonna miss him a lot."[80]

## Testing Positive for Self-Assurance

As in the past, speculation in the media will continue about how success and fame will affect Rose. He is very young to be so prominent and wealthy, and many people in similar positions have run into such serious problems as lawbreaking and substance abuse.

Generally, however, observers have been positive and hopeful in their predictions for Rose's future in this regard. By all accounts, he is more than average in his stability, modesty, focus, and self-confidence.

So far, most of the negative publicity that has surfaced about the athlete's off-duty life has been minor, and it has yet to seriously affect his reputation. Journalist Rick Morrissey is typical of the commentators who have optimistically speculated on

Rose's emotional future. He writes, "Nobody wants to see him turn into the standard-issue, egocentric NBA star. Based on what we've seen so far from this unassuming kid . . . it's hard to envision that happening."[81] Elsewhere, Morrissey comments:

> There's a new calculus [decision-making process] in pro sports. It's not whether a player will get into trouble. It's whether his on-court performance can mitigate [diminish] his off-court problems. . . . Rose doesn't appear to have any issues away from the game, aside from a Gummi Bear habit. . . . This is a kid who regularly tests positive for self-assurance.[82]

## Avoiding Temptations

Especially when he was younger, and early in his pro career, Rose's family continued to protect him from many problems. As he has gotten older, however, he has become more self-sufficient and less in need of outside help.

He still has assistance, though. To augment his brother Reggie's help on the road, for example, Rose hired a former high school coach from Simeon, now a licensed security guard, to be a bodyguard. Rose says that the bodyguard is fun to be around and gives him helpful advice. The protection also lets Rose avoid unwanted attention from people who may want to take advantage of his fame and money.

Although he has thrown his new wealth around, Rose has used it to buy some things for himself and his family. In addition to his home, for example, he treated himself to a luxury car, a Maserati GranTurismo. He also bought his mother a house in suburban Chicago. For one Christmas, he bought her a ring because she missed him while he was on the road. The point guard recalls, "I . . . told her whenever she thinks about me and I'm not there, just look at the ring and I'll always be there."[83]

## "That Will Wear Down on You"

The athlete will also be protected from temptations by the location of his new home in suburban Deerfield. He almost never

*Along with taking care of his family, Rose used his new wealth to buy a few things for himself—including a Maserati Gran Turismo similar to this one.*

goes back to his old neighborhood, preferring to stay in touch with friends by phone, e-mail, and text messages. He comments:

> I think just living [in Deerfield] helps. You have older people out here and younger kids out here, so there's nothing to do . . . but chill in your house and go to a movie or something like that. Other than that, you just focus on basketball.

> It would probably be totally different if I lived in the city, downtown. It's just temptation down there. You always want to go out, [but] I learned early [that] steadily going out, steadily running around, that will wear down on you.[84]

Rose admits that it has been hard to give up hanging out a lot in Englewood: He grew up there, has relatively few bad memories of it, and still has friends there. However, he acknowledges that the shift in his habits was necessary. Rose remarks, "People see me differently now, they see me on a certain stage now and anything can happen."[85]

# Can He Remain Unspoiled?

**M**any observers have expressed the hope that Rose's personality will not change as his pro career continues. They also hope that he will not do anything to taint his reputation, as so many athletes have done. ESPN writer Gene Wojciechowski reflects on this:

> Rose is special. The question is, will he stay that way? . . . I'm talking about the non-hoops Rose. Sports is filled with crater marks from fallen superstars [who have] diluted trust. They made us skeptical and cynical. . . .
>
> Emerging young stars such as Rose don't need to be perfect, they just need to be true to themselves and, if possible, true to sports fans. . . . There are no guarantees Rose will remain unspoiled. Money, fame and a sense of entitlement have ways of anesthetizing common sense. . . .
>
> Five years from now will Rose still look you in the eye? Will his modesty still match his scoring average? In a perfect world, you hope so. But this is a world of imperfections [and] casual and practiced arrogance. It would be nice if Rose, and a few handfuls of other young players could reverse the perception. In fact, it would be better than nice. It would be too good to be true.

Gene Wojciechowski, "Rose an On- and Off-court Success," ESPN.com, May 11, 2009. http://sports.espn.go.com/chicago/columns/story?columnist=wojciechowski_gene&id=4159430.

## A Changed Grade

If Rose is careful and lucky, he will not be the center of serious criticism in the future. However, a celebrity always runs that danger. Despite his efforts to remain low-key and out of the limelight, Rose has already been involved in several controversies.

Some of these have been minor. For example, in 2008 he was found guilty of speeding on an Illinois highway. He was ordered to pay one thousand dollars and attend traffic school. However, considering his age—many young people commit foolish mistakes while driving—few observers considered this a major issue.

More serious was an incident stemming from the athlete's high school days. He was implicated in one of a series of cases in which grades were changed to let athletes maintain their eligibility for college. During his last semester at Simeon, Rose earned a D in one class. The poor grade threatened his chances to attend Memphis, which (like many colleges) requires a minimum high school grade point average.

*Rose and Coach Calipari came under fire when it was rumored that Rose's grades had been changed so he could attend Memphis and that someone else had taken his SAT exam.*

Somewhere along the way, however, Rose's grade was upgraded to a C and stayed that way long enough to make the athlete eligible for the university. The question of who changed the grade has never been completely answered, and the issue of the integrity of the school's grade reporting process is uncertain—as is how much Rose knew about it.

## Cheating on the SAT?

More serious still was a controversy that was also connected to the point guard's move from Simeon to the University of Memphis. In the summer before Rose started his freshman year at college, accusations surfaced that someone else took the athlete's SAT exam in preparation for his admission.

Coach John Calipari has denied any knowledge of wrongdoing. (This is not the first or last time the coach has been implicated in unethical behavior.) For his part, Rose repeatedly denied that he did anything wrong. He stated, "That [accusation] didn't bother me at all, I know I didn't do anything wrong. That was up to Memphis, what they had to do. Coach told me, 'Don't worry about it.' I definitely wasn't worried about it. I was still working out, so I just let [the scandal] pass."[86] The NCAA opened a formal probe into the issue, and in August 2009 it concluded that there had been wrongdoing. The association ruled that Memphis would have to officially cancel all 38 of its wins during the 2007–2008 season, including their trip to the Final Four. Memphis has appealed this decision, arguing that the NCAA clearinghouse had ruled that the athlete had been eligible to play at the time. In March 2010, the NCAA rejected Memphis' final appeal and must vacate the wins.

## A Party Photo Goes Viral

Soon after these accusations were made public, Rose was the center of another controversy. It also dated from his college years. This issue concerned a photo that became public and went viral on the Internet, so that millions of people saw it.

The photo was taken at a party, probably just after the NCAA championship game. It showed the athlete and a friend flashing gang signs. A number of people were outraged. They pointed out that such a photo, even as a joke, was not a good example for a nationally known athlete to set.

In his defense, Rose stated that he cannot remember when it was taken, and that the pose was just for fun. He noted that the

## The Party Photo

**R**ose received negative publicity in 2009 when a photo surfaced and millions saw it on the Internet. In the picture, Rose is throwing signs for the Gangster Disciples Nation, a Chicago gang with tens of thousands of members. In the wake of this mini-scandal, Rose issued the following statement:

> Recently, a photo has been circulating on the Internet which appears to depict me flashing a gang sign. This photo of me was taken at a party I attended in Memphis while I was in school there, and was meant as a joke . . . a bad one, I now admit. I want to emphatically state, now and forever, that Derrick Rose is anti-gang, anti-drug, and anti-violence.
>
> I am not, nor have I ever been, affiliated with any gang and I can't speak loudly enough against gang violence, and the things that gangs represent.
>
> In posing for this picture, I am guilty of being young, naive and of using extremely poor judgment.
>
> I sincerely apologize to all my fans for my mistake. I pride myself on being a good citizen, and role model, that young people can look up to and I want to urge all my young fans to stay away from gangs and gang-related activities.

Quoted in ESPN.com, "Rose: Controversial Photo a Mistake," June 12, 2009. http://sports.espn.go.com/chicago/news/story?id=4252041.

*Rose got in trouble for this controversial photo. In it, he supposedly flashes gang signs.*

period was so hectic and stressful that he cannot even remember the game itself. Rose admits that it was a foolish thing to do, and that he needs to be more careful in the future. He told a reporter, "I'm not a kid anymore. I'm always in a spotlight. [I] gotta be the leader of this team, and I can't do foolish things anymore."[87]

Rose issued a formal statement condemning gang behavior and acknowledging his mistake. The athlete also posted a video on Facebook, thanking his fans for remaining loyal. Then he did his best to move on, telling reporters, "[I] talked to my mom, [she] told me just don't worry about it, and I'm just looking forward to the future."[88]

## Role Model

Embarrassing or regrettable incidents are part of life for virtually every celebrity in the world. In the years to come, Rose will almost certainly be involved in others. However, it will be important for him to keep these to a minimum.

Many commentators continue to express hope that the athlete can learn from his past mistakes. In their opinion, he may not need to completely wall himself off from the everyday world

## In the Back of His Head

Rose gives credit to his mother's early lessons for helping him to avoid serious temptations. Even thinking about his mother, Rose says, is enough to steer him the right way. He remarks, "I think about her any time I do something. I hear her voice. Like, 'Is my Mom going to like this?' or 'How would she react to this?' When I do certain things, she's always in the back of my head."

Quoted in Scoop Jackson, "The Rose That Rose from Concrete," ESPN.com, April 15, 2009. http://sports.espn.go.com/chicago/columns/story?columnist=jackson_scoop&id=4070218.

to avoid publicity. They also believe that he can achieve great things. Sportswriter Jon Greenberg comments:

> I read these stories [about the athlete's controversies] and I feel bad for all those who have lost faith in Derrick Rose and everything they thought he represented. Then I think about where Rose came from, and what he's like as a person, and what kind of man, and role model, he could be one day, and I decide that the dream is still attainable. . . . He can still be everything he wants to be, and most of what we want him to be. But the ball is in his hands now.[89]

Rose would definitely like to continue as a role model for younger athletes. One way to do this, the athlete says, is to visit his old neighborhood occasionally so that young people can meet him. He explains:

> For those kids to see someone [from Englewood] make it is huge because they're not used to seeing famous people or anybody around who's really successful. I hope seeing me can drive them because I know when I was younger, if somebody like me came back to the neighborhood, I would've made sure I remembered that day and I would want to be like that person.[90]

## "The Kid Did It the Right Way"

People who live in Englewood point out that Rose is already having an impact on young people in the neighborhood. For example, David Peterson, a barber who has known the Roses for years, comments, "A lot of the kids in the neighborhood are asking how they can be like Derrick. The kid did it the right way. Go to school. Stay off the corner."[91]

Although he has returned infrequently to Englewood since his rise to the pros, Rose hopes that he will be able to do more to help the neighborhood in the future. For example, he plans to donate significantly to improve his old neighborhood, perhaps by funding improved sports facilities or youth centers. Underwriting a food bank, he says, would be especially significant

*In spite of some controversy, Rose has proven that working hard and avoiding the bad influences in your neighborhood and in your life can bring you success.*

to him. Rose comments, "That's where we used to go get our food when I was young and my mom didn't have enough money."[92]

Rose knows that he will not be able to reach everyone. Some of the people in his old neighborhood will not be open to his message. The point guard says, "They see me doing good, but they think hanging onto the street hustling will get them a better job. I got a couple of friends back there still like that. [But] they just need to believe in themselves like I believed."[93]

One important element in determining Rose's future will be how successful he is in fulfilling his ambitions on the court. He commented to a reporter in the spring of 2009, "I'm not even near a star yet. But hopefully one day I could become one."[94] With good fortune, good health, and his proven athletic skills, Rose's bright future will be a slam dunk.

## Introduction: A Basketball Phenomenon

1. Quoted in Andy Katz, "Rose 'Chases Greatness' with a Passion for Winning," ESPN.com, June 20, 2008. http://sports .espn.go.com/nba/draft2008/columns/story?id=3452587.
2. Quoted in *Springfield (IL) State Journal Register,* "Local Hero Will Be Under Some Serious Pressure," June 27, 2008.
3. Quoted in Brian Landman, "A Timely Blooming," *Chicago Tribune,* April 6, 2008, p. 1.
4. Quoted in Shaun Assael, "Bloomtown," *ESPNmag,* November 26, 2008. http://sports.espn.go.com/espnmag/story?sect ion=magazine&id=3728007.

## Chapter 1: Growing Up in Englewood

5. Quoted in Assael, "Bloomtown."
6. Quoted in Larry Gross, "Beasley Academic Center Proud of Rose," *Chicago Defender,* July 2, 2008.
7. Quoted in Gross, "Beasley Academic Center Proud of Rose."
8. Quoted in Rick Morrissey, "The Kid Did It the Right Way," *Chicago Tribune,* June 27, 2008.
9. Quoted in Bob Sakamoto, "2007 Mr. Basketball of Illinois," *Chicago Tribune,* March 31, 2007.
10. Quoted in Scoop Jackson, "The Rose That Rose from Concrete," ESPN.com, April 15, 2009. http://sports.espn.go .com/chicago/columns/story?columnist=jackson_scoop&id= 4070218.
11. Quoted in *Chicago Sun-Times,* "Derrick Rose," March 2, 2007.
12. Quoted in David Lassen, "Rose Has Become Blossoming Star," *Ventura County (CA) Star,* April 5, 2008. http://pro quest.umi.com.
13. Quoted in Steve Wieberg, "Rose Blooming at Right Time for Memphis," *USA Today,* April 2, 2008, p. C7.
14. Quoted in K.C. Johnson, "The Prize Is Right," *Chicago Tribune,* April 23, 2009.

15. Quoted in Jackson, "The Rose That Rose from Concrete."
16. Morrissey, "The Kid Did It the Right Way." p. 1.
17. Quoted in Lassen, "Rose Has Become Blossoming Star."
18. Quoted in Lassen, "Rose Has Become Blossoming Star."
19. Quoted in K.C. Johnson, "Rose Is No Mystery to Simeon Grad Anderson," *Chicago Tribune*, November 3, 2008. http://archives.chicagotribune.com/2008/nov/3/sports/chi04-bulls-bits-chicagonov4.

## Chapter 2: High School

20. Quoted in John Walters, "Memphis 'Bad Guy' Label Simply Wrong," *Sports Illustrated*, April 7, 2008.
21. Quoted in Lee Goddard, "Rose Blossoms into a Legend," *Corpus Christi (TX) Caller–Times,* April 9, 2008. http://www.caller.com/news/2008/Apr/9/rose-blossoms-into-a-legend/.
22. Quoted in *USA Today*, "Basketball Team," April 18, 2007.
23. Quoted in Scoop Jackson, "Spirit of Former Chicago High School Star Lives on in Rose," ESPN.com, July 1, 2008. http://m.espn.go.com/nba/story?storyId=3469162.
24. Quoted in Brian Hanley, "Miller Gets His Revenge," *Chicago Sun-Times*, December 3, 2008, p. 6.
25. Quoted in Johnson, "Rose Is No Mystery to Simeon Grad Anderson."
26. Quoted in Sakamoto, "2007 Mr. Basketball of Illinois," p. 10.
27. Quoted in Sakamoto, "2007 Mr. Basketball of Illinois," p. 10.
28. Quoted in Sakamoto, "2007 Mr. Basketball of Illinois," p. 10.
29. Quoted in Sakamoto, "2007 Mr. Basketball of Illinois," p. 10.
30. Quoted in Morrissey, "The Kid Did It the Right Way," p. 1.
31. Quoted in Sakamoto, "2007 Mr. Basketball of Illinois," p. 10.
32. Quoted in Katz, "Rose 'Chases Greatness' with a Passion for Winning."
33. Quoted in Andy Katz, "Love, Rose, and Gordon Are Superstars with Realistic Title Hopes," ESPN.com, November 9, 2007. http://sports.espn.go.com/ncb/preview2007/columns/story?columnist=katz_andy&id=3100522.
34. Quoted in Jeffrey Martin, "Rose, Memphis Turned into Perfect Match," McClatchy-Tribune Business News, April 7, 2008.
35. Quoted in Landman, "A Timely Blooming," p. 1.

36. Quoted in Landman, "A Timely Blooming," p. 1.

## Chapter 3: A Year of College

37. Quoted in Andy Katz, "Rose, Griffin Are Comfortable as the Focus of Their Teams," ESPN.com, November 16, 2007. http://sports.espn.go.com/ncb/columns/story?columnist=katz_andy&id=3113271.
38. Quoted in Katz, "Rose 'Chases Greatness' with a Passion for Winning."
39. Quoted in Steve Dilbeck, "This Rose Is Not Done Blossoming," *Los Angeles Daily News*, April 7, 2008.
40. Quoted in Lassen, "Rose Has Become Blossoming Star."
41. Quoted in *Chicago Tribune*, "Deconstructing Derrick; Why Is It So Tough Guardin' Rose?" April 7, 2008, p. 18.
42. Quoted in Corey Green, "Derrick Rose: From Bud to Bloom," *Memphis Tri-State Defender*, March 13, 2008, p. 1.
43. Quoted in Dan Wolken, "Wrapping up APSU," *Memphis Tigers Basketball*, November 29, 2007.
44. Quoted in Katz, "Rose, Griffin Are Comfortable as the Focus of Their Teams."
45. Quoted in Blair Kerkhoff, "Freshman Derrick Rose Has Been a Sensation for No. 1 Memphis," McClatchy-Tribune Business News, January 26, 2008.
46. Quoted in Dana O'Neil, "Rose and CDR Fuel Memphis' Offensive Machine," ESPN.com, April 6, 2008. http://sports.espn.go.com/ncb/ncaatourney08/columns/story?columnist=oneil_dana&id=3332745.
47. Quoted in Teddy Greenstein, "Rose, Beasley Still Just Kids; Writers Share Views of Draft Prospects," *Chicago Tribune*, June 24, 2008, p. 3.
48. Quoted in Landman, "A Timely Blooming."
49. Quoted in Teresa M. Walker, "Memphis: 'Home of the Blues,'" *Oakland (CA) Tribune*, April 9, 2008. http://proquest.umi.com.
50. Quoted in Larry Gross, "Rose Set to Bloom in June NBA Draft," *Chicago Defender*, April 23–29, 2008, p. 53.
51. Quoted in NCAA.com, "Memphis' Rose Going to NBA, Calipari Agrees to Extension," April 15, 2008. www.ncaa.com/sports/m-baskbl/spec-rel/041508aae.html.

## Chapter 4: NBA Rookie Year

52. Quoted in Andy Katz, "Rose Tries to Sway Bulls into Drafting Him Ahead of . . . Beasley?" ESPN.com, June 20, 2008. http://sports.espn.go.com/nba/draft2008/news/story?id=34 52817.

53. Quoted in Chris Colston, "New Bull Attracts a Frenzy All Day Long; Obama: Rose Pick a Slam Dunk," *USA Today*, June 27, 2008, p. C7.

54. Quoted in Gross, "Beasley Academic Center Proud of Rose."

55. Quoted in *St. Louis Post-Dispatch,* "In Draft of Sprouts, Rose Is No. 1," June 27, 2008, p. D3.

56. Quoted in Morrissey, "The Kid Did It the Right Way."

57. Quoted in Gross, "Beasley Academic Center Proud of Rose."

58. Quoted in Mike Dodd, "As NBA Draft Looms, Bulls' Eye Keenly Focused on Rose," *USA Today*, June 26, 2008.

59. Quoted in *NCAA News,* "Rose at Home in 1st Bulls Practice," July 4, 2008.

60. Quoted in K.C. Johnson, "Chicago's Very Own," McClatchy-Tribune Business News, June 27, 2008.

61. Quoted in Mike Dodd, "The Bulls' Eye on Rose," *USA Today,* June 27, 2008, p. C1.

62. Quoted in Marc J. Spears, "Rose Feels Right at Home," *Boston Globe*, November 1, 2008, p. C1.

63. Quoted in K.C. Johnson, "A Thorny Beginning; Rose Learns while Beasley Sings and Scores 28 Points," *Chicago Tribune*, July 8, 2008, p. 3.

64. Quoted in K.C. Johnson, "Memphis Homecoming Has Rose Pumped," *Chicago Tribune*, December 11, 2008, p. 4.

65. Quoted in Johnson, "Memphis Homecoming Has Rose Pumped."

66. Quoted in Fox Sports, "Report: Rose Injured in Bed Eating an Apple," December 12, 2008. http://msn.foxsports.com.

67. Quoted in *Chicago Tribune*, "Red-Faced Rose," December 9, 2008.

68. Quoted in K.C. Johnson, "Chicago Bulls' Derrick Rose Low-Key After Stunning Playoff Debut," *Chicago Tribune*, April 20, 2009. http://proquest.umi.com.

69. Bill Simmons, "Celtics-Bulls Is One for the Ages," ESPN.com, April 23, 2009. www.sport-daily.com/celtics-bulls-is-one-for-the-ages.html.

70. Quoted in Mike McGraw, "Bulls' Rose: The Spotlight Has Been 'Tough,'" *Chicago Daily Herald*, August 6, 2009. www.dailyherald.com/story/?id=312241.

71. Quoted in Mike McGraw, "Rose: 'I'm learning,'" *Chicago Daily Herald*, August 7, 2009, p. 6.

72. Quoted in Colston, "New Bull Attracts a Frenzy All Day Long," p. C7.

73. Quoted in Colston, "New Bull Attracts a Frenzy All Day Long," p. C7.

74. Quoted in John Jackson, "The First Fan Gets to Know the Bulls," *Chicago Sun-Times*, February 27, 2009. http://espn.go.com/blog/truehoop/post/_/id/6013/the-first-fan-gets-to-know-the-bulls.

## Chapter 5: The Future

75. Simmons, "Celtics-Bulls Is One for the Ages."

76. Quoted in Spears, "Rose Feels Right at Home," p. C1.

77. Quoted in Associated Press, "Despite Stomach Issues, Memphis' Rose Will Play in Title Game vs. Kansas," April 6, 2008.

78. Quoted in Rick Morrissey, "On Sound Ground; Rookie Rose Doesn't Have Much to Say, but His Play Sure Has Everyone Talking," *Chicago Tribune*, December 3, 2009, p. 1.

79. Kevin Arnovitz, "What Ben Gordon's Departure Means for Derrick Rose," ESPN.com, July 3, 2009. http://espn.go.com/blog/truehoop/post/_/id/6673/what-ben-gordon-s-departure-means-for-derrick-rose.

80. Quoted in Arnovitz, "What Ben Gordon's Departure Means for Derrick Rose."

81. Morrissey, "Bulls Shouldn't Hold Back Derrick Rose," McClatchy-Tribune News Service, December 7, 2008.

82. Morrissey, "When Bulls Choose, They Can't Lose," *Chicago Tribune*, June 25, 2008.

83. Quoted in Melissa Isaacson, "Bulls' Derrick Rose a Down-to-Earth Rising Star," *Chicago Tribune*, February 14, 2009, p. 8.

84. Quoted in Jackson, "The Rose That Rose from Concrete."

85. Quoted in Jackson, "The Rose That Rose from Concrete."
86. Quoted in McGraw, "Bulls' Rose."
87. Quoted in McGraw, "Bulls' Rose."
88. Quoted in Nick Friedell, "Rose Denies Wrongdoing in SAT Scandal," ESPN Chicago, August 7, 2009. http://sports.espn.go.com/espn/print?id=4381787&type=story.
89. Jon Greenberg, "Controversial Offseason Doesn't Define Rose," ESPN Chicago, June 12, 2009. http://sports.espn.go.com/chicago/columns/story?columnist=greenberg_jon&id=4252642.
90. Quoted in Isaacson, "Bulls' Derrick Rose a Down-to-Earth Rising Star," p. 8.
91. Quoted in Rick Morrissey, "Derrick Rose, the Local Kid Who Made Good," *Chicago Tribune,* June 26, 2008.
92. Quoted in Isaacson, "Bulls' Derrick Rose a Down-to-Earth Rising Star," p. 8.
93. Quoted in Assael, "Bloomtown."
94. Quoted in K.C. Johnson, "Rose: Not Yet in Full Bloom," *Chicago Tribune*, April 2, 2009.

**1988**
Derrick Martell Rose is born on October 4 in Chicago, Illinois.

**2003**
Begins high school at Simeon Career Academy and leads the junior varsity Wolverines to the city championships.

**2004–05**
Starts on the varsity team and again leads his team to the state championships.

**2005–06**
Helps the varsity team win its first state championship since 1984.

**2006–07**
Leads his team to win its second state championship in a row, earns the "Mr. Basketball Illinois" award and many other honors, and graduates from Simeon.

**2007**
Enters the University of Memphis.

**2008**
In June, Rose is chosen as the number-one pick in the NBA draft by the Chicago Bulls.

**2008–09**
On October 28, Rose plays in his first pro game; he finishes his rookie season with the Bulls and wins the Rookie of the Year award.

**ambidextrous**: Able to use both hands.

**double-double:** When a player achieves a double-digit number in two of three categories: points, rebounds, assists, steals, and blocked shots.

**flexor:** A muscle that contracts a joint. Flexors allow people to perform such actions as bending an elbow or knee.

**neurosurgeon:** A brain and nervesurgeon.

**nutritionist:** Someone who specializes in helping people develop healthy eating habits.

**sprain:** An injury caused by twisting or tearing of the ligaments of a joint.

# For Further Reading

## Books

Aaron Frisch, *Chicago Bulls*. Mankato, MN: Creative Education, 2008. A very simple book about Derrick Rose's team, with some nice photos.

John F. Grabowski, *The Chicago Bulls*. San Diego: Lucent, 2003. This book has good background information on the famous team Rose grew up with and plays for now.

Roland Lazenby, *Bull Run: The Story of the 1995–96 Chicago Bulls; The Greatest Team in Basketball History*. Lenexa, KS: Addax, 2002. This book, which has many photos, focuses on the famous last season of Michael Jordan, Derrick Rose's idol.

Mark Stewart and Mike Kennedy, *Swish: The Quest for Basketball's Perfect Shot*. Minneapolis: Millbrook, 2009. This book focuses on the history and development of the game.

## Web Sites

**Chicago Tribune** (www.chicagotribune.com/topic/sports/basketball/derrick-rose-PESPT008549.topic). This site contains many newspaper articles about Derrick Rose as well as photos.

**Derrick Rose Online** (www.derrickroseonline.org). This is a fan site with news, biography, statistics, photos, and more.

**ESPN.com** (http://sports.espn.go.com/nba/players/profile?playerId=3456) This site is maintained by the ESPN network and contains statistics, news, and photos regarding Rose.

**NBA.com** (www.nba.com/playerfile/derrick_rose/). This site has the latest stats on Rose's career.

**Official Site of Derrick Rose** (www.drosehoops.com/rose/index). Rose's official Web site provides a wealth of information, photos, videos, and updates on the Bulls point guard.

Adam Woog is the author of many books for children, young adults, and adults. He lives in Seattle, Washington, with his wife. Both of them wish they could still attend their college-age daughter's high school basketball games.